PLACES

By the same author

AS I SAW THE U.S.A.

SULTAN IN OMAN

SOUTH AFRICAN WINTER

THE HASHEMITE KINGS

THE WORLD OF VENICE

THE ROAD TO HUDDERSFIELD

THE PRESENCE OF SPAIN

CITIES

OXFORD

PAX BRITANNICA

THE GREAT PORT

PLACES

James Morris

A Helen and Kurt Wolff Book
Harcourt Brace Jovanovich, Inc.
New York

For

JULIAN BACH
who got me there

Itinerary

Illustrations

Foreword

The pieces in this small collection are late examples, I think, of a fading *genre*: the travel essay. Now that nearly everyone who reads has been to nearly everywhere there is to read about, the travel writer finds his occupation's gone, and turns to other literary forms—transmuting his experiences into fiction, perhaps, or perhaps like me projecting his view of today into an evocation of yesterday.

It was a *genre* that gave much pleasure in its time, if not to the reader, at least to the fortunate practitioner, for not only by its nature did it offer one a lovely wandering life, but it was also grossly overpaid. For one of my temperament, too, it was an agreeably *slithery* form of expression. I never wished to identify with the objects of my reportage, but following the example of my master Kinglake aspired only to look at them from the outside, detached, unembroiled, and perfectly ready to be stared at in return. My approach was one of guileless irresponsibility; I aimed only to amuse myself, my readers and sometimes my subjects; a few thousand words of prose was the most I generally asked of my Muse, and the most my patrons would print anyway.

I had already exchanged the perpetual theatre of the foreign correspondent's life for these excursions into what used to be called *belles-lettres*: at the beginning of 1972 it became clear to me that my dilettante days were over too, for the writing of travel essays could no longer be relied upon to provide a kind of private income. But I did not mind. I was becoming a different person anyway, I had the world in my head so to speak, and I assembled this collection not as a lament, nor even just as a memento, but as grace after favours.

Trefan, 1972

Acknowledgements

The essay on Malta was first published in *The Architectural Review*, the essays on Ireland and Wyoming in *Encounter*, the essay on Darjeeling in B.O.A.C.'s magazine *Welcome Aboard*. *Holiday* first published those on Alexandria, the Basque country, Iceland and Swaziland, *Life* those on Baden-Baden, Capri, Trouville and Wales, *Venture* those on Chicago, Ceylon, Fiji and Kashmir.

I am grateful to them all for permission to reprint now.

The quotation from C. P. Cavafy's 'At the Café Entrance' on page 22 is reprinted from *The Complete Poems of Cavafy* translated by Rae Dalven published by the Hogarth Press (UK) and Harcourt Brace Jovanovich, Inc (USA) Copyright © 1961 by Rae Dalven.

I thank the following for permission to reproduce photographs in their possession: B.O.A.C., Camera Press, J. Allan Cash, Conway Picture Library, the French Tourist Office, the Irish Tourist Office, Bernard B. Silberstein, the Tourism Council of Greater Chicago and the United States Information Service.

ALEXANDRIA

Our grandfathers, like Baedeker or Napoleon, inspected Alexandria from the front—from the north, from Greece, Italy or the P. and O. Seen from the familiar Mediterranean, the city looks classically self-evident—an ancient and most famous seaport, sweeping spaciously around its bays, and drawn with a Grecian clarity.

From the south, things look very different, for there the port is circumscribed by that queer expanse of brackish water, part salt, part fresh, called Maryût—fragrant with wild flowers in the spring, malodorous in high summer, with fishermen poling themselves about in frail spindly canoes, and boorish fish of monstrous size. A shambled, cluttered townscape is reflected in Maryût, ringed with shacks and railway lines, for here you are seeing Alex out of Egypt. Behind you the desert road has run its forlorn way across the wasteland—nothing since Cairo but a petrol station and a gloomy café: and behind that again all Africa seems to be squatting, breathing its hot breath across the sands.

In the great days of Egyptian travel nobody dreamt of viewing Alexandria from here. This was, to every cultured sightseer, a great city of the Mediterranean, linked indissolubly with Europe by glorious strands of scholarship, celebrated throughout civilization for the schools and libraries of its classical antiquity, its philosophers, astronomers and mathematicians, its associations with men like Euclid, Theocritus, Caesar and even Homer—'there is an island called Pharos in the rolling seas, off the mouth of the Nile'.

Today the rump view is more apposite, and that queer jumbled image in the surface of Maryût is a true paradigm of the place. Alexandria has wrenched itself free of Europe, and disowns the values of the Grand Tour. Cleopatra, Queen of Egypt, has won. Once the second city of the Roman Empire, now this is only a provincial centre of the Arab world, no longer even Egypt's summer capital, only a port and a holiday resort. The marble serenity has vanished, to be replaced by a pungent but violent new energy—the energy of Egypt itself, restless and inconsequential, full of humour but never at peace, like that fevered state of irritable excitement that overcomes people during a sandstorm.

Grandfather's view of Alexandria still has a pathetic majesty. Legend says that Alexander the Great, who personally decreed the shape of the city, is buried somewhere beneath its streets, intact in a crystal coffin, and a few years ago a dedicated Greek waiter arrived from the Piraeus to unearth him. Night and day his fanatic figure was to be seen at work, digging away behind advertising hoardings, peering into manholes, and sometimes so disrupting the traffic by pursuing his researches in the middle of main streets that in the end the tolerant city authorities had to expel him.

For even now there is a magnetism to the old grandeur of Alexandria. Only a few hidden stones are left of the Pharos, seventh wonder of the world, and over them the Arabs long ago built the fort of Qait Bey: but the very knowledge of their existence is enough, and from the imaginary shadow of that metaphysical lighthouse—once 400 feet high, with a gigantic figure of Poseidon on top—the eye sweeps respectfully around one of the grandest of all waterfronts. The corniche at Alexandria is ten miles long, and never seems to peter out: it is lined with block after block of massive four-square buildings, white or sandy-coloured, and is so fuzzed about with balconies that from a distance it seems to be permanently in scaffolding. There is an ex-royal palace at each end: Ras el Tin serene in the west, from whose quay King Farouk sailed away into exile in his own yacht, Montazah flamboyantly in the east, a turreted ogre's lair in a park, set about with lascivious legend.

From one to the other runs that magnificent promenade, with no particular structure to strike the eye, only a fine sweep and a sense of consequence. Alexandria is not a city of notable monuments—'a day', says Hachette's guidebook hopefully, 'is hardly enough for a visit of the city'. But as you stand there in the salty sunshine, with a gusty wind from Asia Minor blowing out of the sea, you can scarcely forget that over there the Canopic Way ran straight as a die between a thousand pillars from the Moon Gate to the Sun Gate, and that in the harbour at your feet Mark Antony's triremes came to anchor. A sentry of the Egyptian Army stands sentinel at Pompey's Pillar, an indeterminate monument of antiquity on a hillock near the station, as if to show that even the severe republicans of modern Egypt retain a respect for the imperial splendours: and when, not long ago, they discovered an enchanting little Greek theatre beneath a building site in the centre of the city, the roughest urchins of the back streets, momentarily tamed by its unearthly grace, were to be seen loitering in silent wonder on the edge of the excavation, gazing down upon that white prodigy beneath.

The scale and some of the pride survive. Alexandria is haunted by superb ghosts—queens, admirals, sages, poets. During the Muslim fast of Ramadan the sunset gun is fired each evening from the mole of Qait Bey: and across the silence of the Eastern Harbour, in that brief pearled hush of the Egyptian twilight, its white puff of smoke drifts mystically and disperses, long after the bang, as though virgins are sacrificing to their gods out there, or they are stoking up the Pharos.

To the post-Baedeker generation, emancipated from pith helmets and classical educations, Alexandria was a city of the nearer Orient— a modern Phoenicia. The concert of this city, as Lawrence Durrell heard it, was polygot and slithery: essentially a Levantine music, sometimes reedy, sometimes harsh, with classical strains to it still, but a soft Arab drum-beat somewhere in the bass.

Thirty years ago this still was a metropolis of the eastern Mediterranean, the capital of Egyptian cotton, the summer capital of the Egyptian government, gifted, wealthy, cynical, with entrepreneurs in sumptuous villas and gilt-collared Consuls-General. Here the peoples of the Levant met to make money, and a dozen jealous national communities lived side by side in the city. All the Powers of the world were represented in this cosmopolitan place, and their Consulates still stand there regretfully, monuments to a lost society. The French gazes sternly across the harbour towards the source of all civilization, f.o.b. Marseilles. The Italian is properly touched with the rococo, an *Aida* in stone. The German has become the local headquarters of the Food and Agricultural Organization, and looks a little priggish. The British towers above the tram terminus, with fine wide terraces for gins and tonics, and shady lawns for bird-watching. Churches of diverse kinds, too, stand witness to old certainties— churches of the Melchites, the Syrians, the Armenians, the Greek Catholics, the Maronites, the Chaldeans, the Scots and the Orthodox Copts, who are in communion with the churches of Ethiopia, and have their own Alexandrine Pope.

These were the several poles of Alexandria, not so long ago, and

Alexandria

around them little worlds separately revolved. Sometimes you may still taste the tang of that vanished city. Sit with some elderly Copt, for example, in the shade of his suburban garden, with a faint smell of jasmine and pomade in the air, and a creak of wicker chairs, and as his clipped dry voice murmurs on, with musty jokes and caustic reminiscences, so you may imagine that the lost society of the pashas still proliferates outside, with all its intricate meshwork of cousin-hoods and family ownership, its cocktails at the Yacht Club and its delicious gossip about the scandals at Montazah. Or accept the chaperonage of one of the young University intellectuals, and allow yourself to be shown the city through a blur of persiflage, *non sequiturs* and comical innuendo—the sly oblique humour of the Levant. Or go to the Patriarchate on a Sunday morning, and watch the Orthodox Copts assembling for worship. The Pope may not be on duty, but the elders of the church will be waiting in turbans and grey gallabiyahs on the cathedral steps, and down their long grave line the worshippers will pass, with respectful handshakes and lowered heads, to disappear into the maw of gold vestments and tinny chanting that is the interior of the fane.

Or stand beneath the plaque that marks the home of C. P. Cavafy, with the traffic rumbling and clanking all around you, and the small boys standing stock still to stare, and you may still be snared by the cadences of that great Greek poet, the laureate of the Levant:

> *Something they said beside me directed*
> *my attention toward the café entrance.*
> *And I saw the beautiful body that looked*
> *as if Eros had made it from his consummate experience—*
> *joyfully modelling its symmetrical limbs:*
> *heightening sculpturally its stature:*
> *modelling the face with emotion*
> *and imparting by the touch of his hands*
> *a feeling on the brow, on the eyes, on the lips.*

One day I entered a restaurant on the corniche to gloat over a copy of Forster's *Guide to Alexandria*, picked up for a fairly expensive song from the library of a dispossessed plutocrat—a handsome signed copy of that rare and delightful work, printed in 1938, and published, as it were out of a dead age, under the auspices of the Royal Archaeological Society of Alexandria. Clutching this treasure, I ordered prawns and Stella beer—and found myself, as I lovingly opened the

Alexandria

yellow covers of the book, miraculously back within its pages, in the 'towsled, unsmartened' Levantine city that Forster knew himself.

A brilliant white sun shone through the windows off the sea, but the restaurant was gently hazed with cigar smoke, steam and cooking fat. It smelt partly of heavy blossom, and partly of shish-kebab. Vases of ageing flowers decorated its tables, dangling glass ornaments hung around its walls, and framed near the door was the statutory price list in Arabic, with fiscal stamps all over it. A dark bored girl in a blue blouse sat dispiritedly at the cash desk. Distracted waiters rushed about with trays, like a chorus of barmen in a musical.

And all around me the Greeks were at their food. Their mothers-in-law were there in fustian black. Their children were there in elaborate frills. A sprawling family unit sat slunched over its victuals at each table, talking loudly in Greek with its mouths full, greeting friends with expansive napkined gestures, and sometimes abruptly propelling small boys in tight-buttoned suits towards the lavatories behind the velvet curtain. With that light, and those prawns, and the thick Arabic cries that came from the kitchen quarters, and the tinkle of those glass beads when a gust of wind came through the door— with E. M. Forster beside me on the tablecloth that day, I could be nowhere else in the world but Alexandria.

But melancholy ruled—with the fiscal stamps. Animated though the scene was, those Greeks seemed dispossessed. The city outside was no longer theirs, and their world had shrunk with the centuries, smaller and smaller from the great Hellenic world of the ancients, to a plate of pilaf with the children on Saturday. Levantine Alexandria is a shabby white city now, its sensuality dulled, its sybarites long since banished or reformed. Its sun is white, its walls are dingy white, even its remarks are pallid with nostalgia. 'Ah, you should have been here twenty years ago!' Or: 'Before the war, now, this was the happiest city in the world—and look at us now!' Or, most inescapably of all, that plaintive inquiry of the ill-used everywhere: *'What have we done to deserve it?'*

Alexandria has lost its old meaning and panache, and the great European communities of the place are dwindled or subdued. The café life of Alex, which once linked this city so intimately with the mores of southern Europe, is almost dead, and the coffee houses themselves, once alive with prattling matrons, nannies and essayists, are now reduced to frayed stained tablecloths, weedy flower-beds

23

beneath the trellises, and waiters pottering desultorily about with feather brushes.

The streets around the Cotton Exchange were once an affluent amalgam of commerce and high finance, cramped heavy thoroughfares with small expensive shops—'something of the brilliant narrowness of Bond Street', Ronald Storrs thought in 1905. Now the Exchange itself is peeling and deserted, with vast political slogans often attached to its façade, and a glowering policeman with a rifle outside its doors; and those once-enticing streets are sadly faded, stocked with Egyptian-made toothpastes and greyish indigenous fashions. Maybe after two hours', is the mechanical reply of the concierge at the Cecil Hotel, when he is asked when the water will be coming on: and somewhere upstairs there lives one last old English couple, relics of the summery thirties—the wife blind and bed-ridden, the husband still sometimes to be encountered descending the dark staircase with a careful soldierly tread.

Only a few of the tarboosh shops survive, their brass moulds glimpsed through clouds of ironing steam, and the palatial waiting rooms of the British Consulate-General, where once the cotton magnates impatiently thrummed the table, are now haunted mostly by poor Maltese, demanding their passports. The past is gliding into literature. I went to the Greek cemetery to look for Cavafy's grave, and was received most courteously by an elderly guardian sitting on a chair outside the mortuary chapel. He took me to the register of burials kept in a cupboard behind the altar, and ran his finger conscientiously through the quill-pen list of names, murmuring their polysyllables under his breath: but in the end he had to close the book with a reverent thud, and confess himself defeated. Cavafy, that solitary genius of Levantine Alexandria, was forgotten. 'Was he a local man?' the caretaker asked me sympathetically. 'The name seems familiar.'

The palm trees in Liberation Square are layered with dust, as though they need a good brush-down, and all over the Levantine city an air of seedy neglect lies like a blight. Many a side-street seems to be plunged in perpetual siesta, and the visitor wandering off the main thoroughfares will suddenly find himself crossing the bar of a stagnant, silent, private backwater, listlessly declining there in the afternoon. The drain-hatches are blocked with sand and dust. The pavement slabs are irregularly tilted. Three or four men are drinking

Alexandria

coffee on the sidewalk, straddling their chairs and exchanging sporadic gloomy grunts. Outside his door lounges a single prickly Greek, sucking a cheroot and wearing a shirt with a brass collar-stud, but no collar. On a balcony high above a woman in a pink housecoat yawns, looks languidly right and left, runs her fingers through her hair and lights a cigarette. A shrouded scavenger, muffled eerily about the head, scuffles about for fag-ends, and at the end of the shadowy little street the blinding sun stands there like an insulating wall, criss-crossed with trams.

Beggars still infest the centre of Alexandria, and chill the susceptible stranger with compassionate loathing. I was walking home in Alex one evening when I felt, rather than actually saw, a legless beggar observing my passage from across the street. He was strapped to a low wooden trolley, which he pushed along with his hands, and made an object at once heart-rending and abhorrent to see: but I had no money on me, neither a pound nor a piastre, so I quickened my step self-consciously and hurried down Zaghloul Street towards my hotel.

Behind me I could hear the whirr of his roller-skate wheels, as he pursued me through the town—a thump when he eased himself off the sidewalk, a clanking when he crossed the tramlines, a change of pitch when he left the tarmac for the flagstones. Faster and faster I walked through the evening crowds, but I could never escape those whirring wheels: over the low wall into Zaghloul Square: across the little garden, and I could hear them skidding down the path, closer than ever behind my back, so that I could hear the poor man's panting breath, too; until at last, breaking into a run, I threw myself into the revolving door of the Cecil. The wheels came to a sudden stop on the sidewalk outside, and a curse bade me good night.

Legendary on the seafront; torpid in the centre; the vitality of Alexandria is all at the back. The pallor of this city is the pallor of a hiatus—a pause in history, at a point where civilizations meet. Europe has withdrawn from this African seaport, leaving nostalgia and bitterness behind: but from the back Egypt herself comes flooding in, like fresh blood into desiccated veins—as though Maryut itself has burst its banks, and is inundating the city with muddy life. Baedeker's view and Durrell's music are both illusory now: today you must look at Alex out of the desert, and allow for a lot of noise.

'The Arab town' or 'the Native quarter' is what they used to call

Alexandria

the cluttered area between the harbours, where only the most scabrous sort of European normally lived. From Qait Bey it only shows as a kind of blur in the grand symmetry of the waterfront, as though your binoculars are not in focus: but when you enter Alex by way of Maryût, it greets you with indescribable colour, vigour, squalor and variety. Then you know you are entering an Islamic city of Africa, conquered long ago by Arabs—a city that cares little for Athens or Imperial Rome, but is related by blood or religion to Baghdad, Amman and even Addis Ababa. Its energy is terrific, its face is unbeautiful, and already it seems to overawe the faded streets of the Levantine bourgeoisie.

It is mostly a maze of crumbled mud streets, tall overhanging tenements with filthy sidewalks, sordid in the daytime, evocatively sinister at night, like the ill-lit lanes of a medieval European city. In and out the winding alleys go, with powerful suggestions of rats and pox, with silent watchmen sitting on stools in dark doorways; and sometimes, through a half-open door, you may see flitting white figures in lamp-light, like pale hallucinations, or unhappy infant whores. Sometimes there is a sudden splurge of Arab voices, shrill and vicious above the roar of the city, as though behind those shuttered casements some crime of deviate passion has just been committed. Sometimes there is a sizzle of cooking-fat from a backyard, or a sudden flash of laughter and smiles, as a covey of raggety children darts out of one alley and into another.

Every now and then the labyrinth abruptly opens into a full-blown Arab square—deafening and tumultuous, spiced, dirty, genial and desperately over-crowded. The white mass of a mosque rises on the background, illuminated by the street lights, and out of every window the radios seem to blare, perpetually fortissimo, with fruity announcers' voices and slithery nasal quarter-tones. All is nervous noise and movement—sidewalk buskers, sweetmeat sellers, sailors with dirty books and hilarious students shooting at explosive caps with airguns at sidestalls. Ramshackle taxis rock and shudder across the square. Single-decker trams pull double-decker trams through the babel. Army officers in padded greatcoats step from official cars and disappear portentously into tenements. Down narrow bazaars, ablaze with light, you may glimpse a shimmer of pots and pans, a violence of yellow nylon, stacks of pop bottles and trays of wizened herbs.

Where the Arab Quarter meets the sea the graceful boats of the fishermen, felucca-rigged, lie aslant upon the shingle. It is as though

Alexandria

the Egyptians have forced their way through to the Mediterranean, cutting a corridor among the aliens. Today the whole quarter seems to be expanding like a ghetto set free—spilling across the corniche, where the little Egyptians race each other precariously along the parapet, overwhelming the haughty purlieus of Ras el Tin, seeping around the forlorn Cotton Exchange towards the grand suburbs of the east. One day, I do not doubt, this irresistible vigour will revivify all Alexandria in a coarser kind, and the city will look out across the Mediterranean with an altogether different confidence—not as she used to, with an almost proprietorial bow towards Europe, but far more assertively, as something new and powerful out of Africa.

So expectancy tempers dejection, and one dynamic succeeds another. I was wandering the streets of the Arab Quarter one day—'the best way to see it,' Forster says, 'is to wander aimlessly about'—when I happened to catch the eye of a wrinkled cabby with a towel wrapped round his head, high behind his poor Rosinante on the seat of his garry. On the impulse of the moment I winked: and instantly there crossed his face an expression of indescribable knowingness and complicity, half comic, half conspiratorial—as though between us, he, the city and I, we had plumbed the depths of human and historical experience, and were still coming wryly up for more.

BADEN-BADEN

South from Frankfurt runs one of the busiest roads in Europe, the first of the autobahns, which pounds its way towards Switzerland in a turmoil of trucks, winking lights and strained nerves. Past Darmstadt and Mannheim it goes, past the hill of Heidelberg and the towers of Karlsruhe, into the thicket country of the Black Forest: until there discreetly detaches itself, all among the woods, the road to Baden-Baden. The traveller who takes this turn will feel a kind of insulation forming around him, a serenity altogether separate from the thrust of the great highway behind his back. Baden-Baden is a small spa town, set in a narrow parklike valley among wooded hills. It became famous as a rendezvous of pleasure for the grandees of nineteenth-century Europe, and its declared purpose today is to relive those spacious, opulent and fragrant days, three miles off the autobahn.

Its tradition as a spa is at least as old as the Romans, who found here one of the hottest chloride springs in Europe, and made the site of Baden-Baden a popular rest camp for the legions. Its tradition as a resort of the monied aristocracy is essentially Victorian, and scarcely feels stale today. Baden-Baden has been gently treated by history—since 1689 no battles have scarred it, nor even bombs. It is blessed with a bland and preservative climate, which brings the flowers out, so its publicists like to say, earlier than they bloom in Lugano. Visually the little town has not much changed since the days of the last century's print-makers, for whom it formed a favourite subject. The lawns are still as green, the little rococo theatre is still as florid; the steaming mineral water still spouts from the beak of the iron stork in Sofienstrasse; the Russian church still has its onion dome; the royal stand at the Iffezheim racecourse still looks like the poop of some high and dry old steam yacht; and through that pleasant setting there still wander, if not the discredited patricians of the *Almanach de Gotha*, at least many a steel-magnate from Düsseldorf, many a leathery Manhattan heiress, and a few sight-seers who look more or less like dukes.

Baden-Baden

Though it flourished earlier, Baden was chiefly a product of the spacious European unity that succeeded the Napoleonic wars: only a patina of unity, imposed upon the patchwork Continent by the mesh of royalties that then dominated it—Hohenzollerns and Romanoffs, Hapsburgs and Bourbons, kings of Württemberg and grand dukes of Saxe-Weimar—families infinitely subdivided, so that Germany was littered with kings and petty princes, and to this day the Margrave of Baden-Baden is nephew to the Duke of Edinburgh, cousin to the King of Greece, and brother-in-law to Prince Tomislav of Yugoslavia. The German nobility decreed the standards of this dynastic Europe, but the French set its style, and it was a Frenchman, Jacques Benazet, who took over the Casino of Baden, built its theatre, and made it one of the most exclusive resorts in Europe. In no time at all the kings and queens were enthusiastic patrons, and were building all over the little town those heavy, sad and bourgeois villas for which the international rich have always cherished such an inexplicable preference.

They did not all come for the gambling. Nor did they all want the treatment, famous though the Baden cure became. The magnetism of the place was, so to speak, self-generating: the more they came, the more they were followed. So smart did Baden become that the Parisians called it their summer capital. The delightful Lichtentaler Allee, along the banks of the little river Oos, was one of the most fashionable of all avenues, where equipages rivalled one another in dazzle and dressage, where the dashing Prince Menshikov clattered past behind the white horses of his troika, and an eccentric horse-breeder called Hammelweiss, wearing a hat with a long tassel, sat hunched in a cart pulled by four billy goats, with dogs yapping all about and flags flying behind. Concerts were regularly attended, so the papers of the time complacently reported, by *l'élite de l'aristocratie européene*, and where the nobs went, so went the Morgans and the Vanderbilts, the courtesans and the adventurers—and the artists. Brahms visited Baden, Berlioz wrote an opera for its theatre, Turgenev built himself a mansion on its hillside, Dostoevsky lost his shirt there, and even Goethe, we are wistfully told, would have visited the town if the axle of his carriage had not broken on the way from Heidelberg.

Between them all, they made of it a formidably grand little pleasure dome, exceedingly knowledgeable about protocol and pedigree, embellished with sculptured stags, cherubs and muses, and inhabited

Baden-Baden

at its climax, it is said, by 300 families entitled to call themselves
'princely'. The grand duke of Baden, who reverted to the title of
margrave after the Second World War, was then a proper sovereign
of an autonomous state, and he was host at one time or another to
most of his peers. Queen Victoria loved the town—its air was 'so
becoming'. The Kaiser Wilhelm I went there for forty years running.
The last czar took his family there. The inns that had once provided
homely lodgings for rheumatic patients now flaunted fancy names
like Hotel de l'Europe, or Hotel de la Ville de Paris, and César Ritz
himself worked at the Brenners Park. For the Baden season of 1870,
actors, dancers and singers were summoned from Paris, Vienna,
Lisbon, Madrid, London and St. Petersburg. Among the competitors
in the first Baden tennis tournament (the game had been introduced
by the parson of the Anglican church) was the future Edward VII of
England. Such was Baden in its prime—very rich, very grand, and so
sure of itself that it had no compunction in aggrandizing its own name,
to differentiate itself from lesser spas: *baden* means merely 'baths',
but since 1900 Baden-Baden has been doubly so.

It lost its splendour, as so many of its princely houses lost their
meaning, in 1914. It had survived the Franco-Prussian War, only
becoming less French and more Prussian. It had evaded, in 1872, the
banning of public gambling in Germany: the sporting set merely
formed itself into a fearfully exclusive society, the International
Racing Club, and set up its own tables in a mansion first built for the
Queen of Sweden, and then acquired from one of the Rothschilds.
Sarajevo, however, stunned Baden-Baden. Among those doused lights
of Europe were the chandeliers of this famous place, so proudly repre-
sentative of a world that would never revive. They still preserve
the visitors' book of the vanished Messmer Hotel, for nearly half a
century the Kaiser's favourite (he slept on a camp bed there). Kings
and queens of Naples have signed it, the Princes of Wales, the Grand
Duchess Anastasia of Russia, Franz Liszt and Chancellor Bismarck:
but it ends in 1914, and its final signature is Von Moltke's.

Baden-Baden prospered intermittently between the wars, but had
lost its cachet. In 1933 Hitler even legalized public gambling there
again—he needed the foreign currency—and the Casino, alone in
Germany, actually stayed in business until 1944. Baden-Baden's overwhelming interest now, though, is an attempt by the new Germany,
that phenomenon of cash and technology, to re-create its lost past of

fountains, princelings and romantic charm. The old school tranquillity of Baden-Baden is as conscious a creation of showmanship as the Tivoli Gardens in Copenhagen, or Disneyland in California. In a Europe half socialist, Baden-Baden deliberately cultivates the grand manner. Some of the hotel rooms at its spa are reserved for patients who go there at the expense of the state, but one suspects that any higher proportion of such trade would not be altogether welcome. There are, after all, many other spas: in Baden-Baden it's the tone that counts.

This is a precarious tightrope to tread: between the mawkish and the ostentatious, in a Germany where *nouveau-riche* values are riding high, and snobs are two a pfennig. Baden, however, gracefully reaches the other side. This is partly because the place is run by men who understand the risks of taste involved, and partly because there survives in Baden-Baden, a gift from the idyllic wine country by which it is surrounded, a refreshing kind of simplicity. In some parts of Germany there is something baleful in the wide-eyed innocence of the people: in Baden-Baden it is all beguilement, and shows itself chiefly in a nice decorum and a transparent desire to please.

At a price, of course. The very point of Baden-Baden is its nostalgic swank—touched up indeed by every modern technique, from slot machine tights to Interpol at the Casino, but still rich in period flavour: the gilded boxes of the theatre, only awaiting their ribbons and tiaras; the suites, like the rooms of some lovely country house, in the sumptuous Brenners Park (where clients often weigh themselves before dinner, to see how many courses they can afford to eat); the ornate old gas-lamps, still lit by a lamp-lighter in a white coat, outside the Kurhaus; the pump room where all Europe's newspapers await you, fresh that day from Oslo, Rome or London; the meticulously tended gardens that line the little Oos (in whose water live trout so genteel that the most ruffianly poacher would scarcely presume to tickle them).

The Casino remains a very picture of nineteenth-century magnificence, for all the plump businessmen who, glazed but seldom inattentive, gamble for huge stakes with the gold and silver jetons they use at week-ends: all is plush, cut glass, and Versailles gilding, the croupiers paragons of genial efficiency, the chuckers-out invisible, the supervisors wise as Wimbledon umpires on their high chairs, and the director of the place just as proud of it, and in just the same tone of voice, as the head of an orphanage, say, or a professor of Slavonic philology with a new faculty building. There is to every casino something suggestive of a very expensive brothel, as you step through its haughty doors into the perfumed privacy inside: but at Baden-Baden, where the coffee is excellent and fruit machines are forbidden with a fastidious shudder, it does at least feel as though Madame may be the Pompadour herself, and all her young ladies the relicts of long-decapitated noblemen.

The Casino is the core of Baden-Baden. Even its superbly organized but somehow creepy bath establishment, where the masseurs move about with a muscular tigerish tread, and the businessmen lie huge and hairy flat on their backs in the steam room—even that hushed temple feels ancillary to the roulette wheels, the orchestras, the plays and the exquisite boutiques that cluster around the Kurhaus. Once you leave those magic precincts, however, you will find the sophistication of it all mercifully fading. First come the gardens, where old ladies in felt hats and numberless chiffon scarves stoop to identify unfamiliar specimens; then there are the cobbled streets of the old city, with steep-pitched roofs as in fairy tales, and smells of sausages and coffee; and finally, scarcely outside the limits of the little town, lies the gentle countryside of the Black Forest, a landscape whose legends are full of ghosts and giants, but whose character is essentially benevolent, and whose inhabitants seem to subsist very satisfactorily on trout, deer steak, and wine out of the garden.

This serenity of setting saves Baden from absurdity, and tempers its pretensions. The place has had its ups and downs since the days of the Hohenzollerns, and has welcomed some variegated modern visitors. Hitler went there once, and is said to have been so offended by a rude noise from a bystander that he never went again. Pétain and Laval both hid in Baden-Baden when life became too much for them. The unhappy neutral embassies, withdrawn from Berlin near the end of the war, lived at the Brenners Park with a sedative plenitude of wine and two choices of luncheon daily, while the Reich to which they were accredited disintegrated around them. The Mexicans have a consulate in Baden-Baden, the Ambassador of Haiti has an official residence. Furtwängler died in the town. The monarchs of earlier times have mostly been replaced by autocrats of commoner stock, but the tourist department is still proud to boast the patronage of an Arabian king or a Persian empress.

And the charm miraculously survives with the decorum. Baden-Baden's market is held in the square outside the big Catholic church

Baden-Baden

called the Stiftskirche. It is a happily bucolic affair, with stalls of potted plants, piles of rich vegetables, and jolly countrywomen in head scarves: and standing paternally above it, supervising its trans-actions with a properly magisterial air, stands the castle, hereditary home of the Baden grand dukes. They have lived in this town for several centuries, and the museum is full of the cuirasses, jerkins and top-boots that their own armies used to wear before the unification of Germany (the dragoons had a big brass letter B on the front of their feathered helmets). More than most German towns, Baden-Baden has enjoyed stability, and it still seems to know its place. The margrave is spoken of with respect. His father is well remembered. The lamp-lighter bows to the spa director, and the spa director removes his hat to the lamplighter. The president of the International Racing Club, which still runs the exceedingly suave August race meeting, is, I need hardly say, Prince Eugene of Oettingen-Wallerstein. Stamps may be swapped at the Philatelic Society on the first and last Mondays of every month, and the police station, so the guide-books endearingly tell us, is closed on Saturdays. The young people of Baden-Baden, when they have one of their dances in the great hall of the Kurhaus, behave with an elegant restraint: and the horse-cabs that still ply these streets move around on pneumatic tyres to avoid disturbing the dowagers.

For Baden-Baden is among towns as the old *Queens* were among steamships: an institution where premiums are frankly placed upon propriety, service and lineage. I suppose wild young men do go there to fizzle away fortunes at the gaming tables, and there is certainly a clique of smart young residents in loud sports cars and dark glasses. Sometimes the emphasis on present wealth and past grandeur does strike one as false and unhealthy. For the most part, though, Baden-Baden is a spacious, leisurely, considerate little town, a place of flowers and cream cakes and glorious church bells—the kind of haven, as the brochures say of its spa, that can provide a cure for 'the ail-ments of civilization'.

By civilization they mean, of course, all that rumpus on the auto-bahn, and it is true that if you keep your eye open for the proper exit you can temporarily be cured. In Baden-Baden there are ninety-four registered doctors: but the real therapists of the spa are those old dukes, maharajas, emperors and grand duchesses, whose lordly favours elevated Baden-Baden long ago, and have left it calm and courtly still when all their dynasties have crumbled.

BASQUE
COUNTRY

As the traveller approaches the western foothills of the Pyre-nees, whether he is coming from the French side or the Spanish, he is likely to notice something funny happening to the street signs. Some very odd names are creeping in. Xs and Zs abound in the patronymics of greengrocers, villages become less pronounceable with each passing mile, and for once the fading syntax of a classical education is no help at all. The stranger may be forgiven for supposing, as he hastily avoids the turning to Itxassou or Oxocel-haya, that he has somehow strayed off the map of Europe, and is entering some separate and more esoteric continent.

In fact he is entering the country of the Basques, a separate and distinctly esoteric people. Some of them are French by nationality, some Spanish, and they live on both flanks of the Pyrenees: but through all the vicissitudes of European history they have maintained their own character, their own appearance, their own customs and above all their own words. Any description of the Basques must begin with their language, just as any introduction to their homeland starts with those arcane road signs, for the Basques more than anyone depend upon their language for their existence as a race. Without it they would long ago have been absorbed into wider racial patterns. With it they have remained one of the most pungent and forcible minorities in Europe, one of the very few small races of the West to defy all the threats and briberies of ethnic conformity.

Basque is one of the world's more alarming languages. Only a handful of adult foreigners, they say, have ever managed to learn it. The Devil tried once and only mastered three words—profanities, I assume. Basque is apparently related to no other language, except perhaps one of the lesser Hungarian dialects. It has a congested look to it, is technically described as agglutinative and polysynthetic, and is full of preoccupied words like *Lerdokiztatu, Edantxar* or *Xintxuketa*. One must think in an altogether different way, to talk Basque, for each transitive verb has fourteen different forms; one word means

Basque Country

'she gives it to him', another 'they give it to us', another 'you give it to them', not to speak of those for 'she will give it to us', or 'you would have given it to me' or even (I suppose, for I am getting out of my depth now) 'it might have been given by us to her'. To make a plural in Basque you add the suffix k. The Basque word for 'philanthropy', my dictionary tells me, is *Gizadi-Ontzaletasun*. The Basque word for 'almost' is *Ya-Ya*.

I am hardly qualified to write about the Basques, because I do not understand this nerve-wracking language: but as no other English-speaking professional writer understands it either, I fear you will have to make do with me.

The Basques inhabit a moist bumpy country on the shores of the Bay of Biscay. Of the seven traditionally Basque provinces, three are in France, four in Spain: perhaps half a million Basques are Spanish citizens, and another 100,000 Frenchmen. The Basque ethos is strongest in the Spanish coastal provinces of Guipúzcoa and Vizcaya, and it peters away gradually east, west and south, the language fading, the customs losing their tang, under the influence of France and Castile. On the perimeters the Basque are scarcely distinguishable as a people. In the centre they are absolutely unmistakable.

They achieve a daily summit of Basqueness on the waterfront of San Sebastian, the provincial capital of Guipúzcoa. This is an international resort, full of snobbery and starched nursemaids, and for a couple of months in high summer it is actually the capital of Spain, the Government moving up from Madrid in haughty panoply. It is also, though, a busy Basque fishing port, and along the esplanade from the grand hotels the fishing people conduct their affairs with an old and earthy gusto. The trawlers side-step skilfully through the narrow harbour entrance, their stocky crews cast to a Victorian mould of seamanship. The longshoremen clatter about with high-wheeled barrows full of ice. Shuddering diesel trucks load up with lobsters, mullet or baby eels for the insatiable gourmets of Madrid. On the quayside, any morning when the catch comes in, the Basque fishwives sit at auction.

There are few more formidable sights in Europe than a full-blooded San Sebastian beldame selling fish upon that water-front. Tourists gape, policemen sheepishly perambulate, fishermen in blue denims trundle to and fro with trays of fish, a calculating throng of restaurateurs and fishmongers sucks its pencils and fingers its wallets:

Basque Country

and in the centre of it all, supreme, unchallengeable, Basque woman-hood enormously presides.

The auctioneer is flanked by cronies, sitting brawnily on kitchen-chairs like a gangster's bodyguard. She herself stands in the middle with a microphone around her neck, wearing a blue anorak, a pink chiffon scarf, white ankle socks and a suggestion of innumerable underclothes. She is in her sixties, perhaps, and looks as though no nuance of life has escaped her. Her face is heavy-jowled, her wrists are very muscular, and she is built like a boxer, but there is a rich urbanity to her voice as she intones the price of the sardines. The crowd is altogether at her command. The seamen stumble in with their fish-trays like acolytes in an archiepiscopal presence. The cronies laugh at every joke. The policemen shuffle about. The customers never dare to argue. But sometimes that empress of the fish-market, pausing to scribble a price upon her pad, notices a baby in some-body's arms, and looks up unexpectedly with the sweetest of grand-motherly smiles, a twiddle of cod-scaled fingers and what I take to be the Basque equivalent of 'Iddums-didums'.

I know of no exact equivalent to this character anywhere else in the world (her nearest relatives are perhaps the bowler-hatted market-women of Bolivia). She seems to be at once Gothic and Latin, with a perceptible oriental streak as well. In a Catholic region of traditional piety, where men and women still sit separately in church, she appears to be altogether emancipated. Across the harbour from one of the most sophisticated resorts in Europe, she might have swaggered straight out of some medieval tavern. In all this she is very Basque. Nobody quite knows who the Basques are, or how they first came to their corner of the Pyrenees. They are of distinctive appearance—dark, thick, beak-nosed—and highly individual character: and like the fishwife, they seem to have no peers.

They are an able people—money-people, organizers, builders and great sailors. On the French side of the Pyrenees the Basque country is mostly pastoral, conveniently laced with tourism. On the Spanish side its tone is set by the great iron-fields around Bilbao, the basis of many industries and an economic mainstay of Spain. On both sides the atmosphere is one of astute competence—the kind of acumen that does not bother with fiddly details, checking a passport or charging for a tyre valve, but drives straight to the profitable heart of things, an immediate trade-in price or a meeting with the board of directors

Basque Country

at eleven o'clock sharp. Few cities of southern Europe are so punctual and industrious as Bilbao, the economic capital of the Basques, where every other building seems to be a bank, and eight miles of river front clank with derricks, ships and warehouses. The Hispanophile must look elsewhere for his orange-blossom idylls: Bilbao is more like Hamburg than Seville, and in its restaurants groups of businessmen perpetually discuss the stock prices, in sober grey suits over plates of eel-spawn.

The Basques have been historically successful at enterprises requiring drive more than meditation—garlic, as their cooks prefer it, more than thyme. They were organized whalers at least as early as the twelfth century, their boats ranging clear across the Atlantic to the Newfoundland grounds, and throughout their history they have been tremendous explorers and colonizers. The first man to sail around the world was a Basque, Juan Sebastian Elcano, who took over the command when Magellan died in the Philippines. Simon Bolivar was a Basque, and so was de Lesseps of the Suez Canal. The two supreme Basque saints were both men of forceful initiative: St. Francis Xavier, who took the Cross to Japan, and St. Ignatius Loyola, first general of the Jesuits. Basques have always been excellent settlers, always ready to travel: their colonies thrive still in Mexico, in Nevada and on the River Plate, and a familiar sight of the southern French roads is another bus-load of Basques bouncing in their black berets, stacked around with packages and baskets, towards the profitable opportunities of Paris.

On the high and gloomy pass of Roncevalles, between France and Spain, I sat on the grass one afternoon and read the legend of Roland's death: for it was through this morose defile that Charlemagne and his knights withdrew from Spain in 778, savaged by the vindictive locals, and somewhere up here that the chivalrous Roland fought his last. It all seemed very close to me: the giants and the magic swords, the noble knights and the chargers, the call of the great horn Olivant which plucked the birds dead from their flight: and closest of all, I uncomfortably thought, the black shaggy forms of the Basque guerrillas, whooping weirdly out of the sun and rolling gigantic boulders down the mountain-sides.

If the Basques were bloody-minded then, they are hardly more tractable today. Their most noted characteristic down the ages has been a fierce independence. They rolled stones on Charlemagne, they disconcerted Wellington, they were among General Franco's toughest opponents in the Spanish Civil War. If you drive towards the coast from Bilbao, through the lush foothills of Vizcaya, swathed in dark green timber and speckled with white farms, presently you will come to a small market town in a valley—cosily settled there, with kerchiefed women working in its fields as in the travel posters, and the scudding clouds of this Atlantic shoreline driving their shadows up and down the valley floor. It looks at first sight like many another Basque town, neither untowardly ugly nor exceptionally attractive, but you may recognize the name emblazoned at the civic limits: Guernica.

Guernica has been from time immemorial the shrine of Basque liberties. It is their Runnymede. Under the ancient Spanish kings the Basques won for themselves a condition of semi-independence: they elected their own representatives, village by village, to an assembly that met in the shade of a symbolic oak tree in Guernica, and each Spanish king swore upon his accession to respect the privileges of the Basques. Every Basque was officially a nobleman, though the nobility did not always show: as the Englishman Richard Ford wrote in the 1840s, 'although the Basque Provinces may typify the three Graces of Spain, the natives sacrifice but little to maintain those types of amiable humanity'.

The Spanish Basques lost most of their privileges when they rose against the Spanish Crown in the Carlist war of the 1830s, and they lost the rest when they backed the losing side in the Spanish Civil War. As for the French Basques, they long since sank their fortunes in those of France. Even so, nationalist feeling rides high on both sides of the frontier. 'We are a nation', you will be told, 'not a region, not a group of provinces, not a language, not a folk tradition, but a nation, Euzkadi, the nation of the Basque'. For a few months at the beginning of the Spanish Civil War this resolution was actually embodied in a Basque Republic, formed of three Spanish provinces: it was established after a plebiscite with the blessing of the Republican Government in Madrid, and it had its own stamps and currencies, its flag, its President and all the protocol of sovereignty.

Its memory lingers, and in France there is still, thirty years later, a sad assembly of politicians calling itself the Basque Government in Exile. In houses and museums, or among the bric-à-brac of conversation, you may still trip over relics of its brief pride: a faded patriotic poster, with a virile young Basque in a beret, chest out on a hillside; or a queer forgotten banknote at the back of a drawer, about as worthless as a currency can be; or an old soldier's tale of the ramparts before Bilbao, when Franco's cavalry was storming up from the south. Or you may still see for yourself the sacred oak tree of Guernica.

Hitler's bombers, flying on Franco's behalf, destroyed the centre of Guernica one afternoon in April, 1937, in an exploit which was to disturb the conscience of the world. The burning of the town symbolized the end of Basque independence. When, after the Civil War, the Basque Provinces were re-united with Franco's Spain, all vestiges of the old privileges were expunged. Navarre, historically another Basque province, had fought on Franco's side, and was rewarded with an unusual degree of autonomy: the three northern provinces had fought for the Republicans, and they were treated as conquered territories.

In the event Basqueness has proved indestructible, and though General Franco has never restored the privileges of the Basques, his regime has perceptibly relaxed its old disapproval of the language. This is partly because Madrid has come to recognize the tourist appeal of regional cultures, but chiefly because the Basques themselves, led often by their priests, have kept their racial loyalty intact. In France and in Spain the Basques argue on. In Spain one hears of rallies broken up by the police, fiery sermons, priests imprisoned, strikes that are really nationalist protests. In France, where nobody is going to lock you up for your opinions, a slogan commonly scrawled on railway bridges is *Euzkadi* 7 = 1 — a gnomic plea for the union of the seven Basque provinces.

So Guernica retains the wistful allure of might-have-been. For centuries its heart was the oak tree, the supreme token of Basque nationality, beneath whose hoary boughs the elected elders of the nation met in legislature. Successive oaks have been destroyed and planted, but there have been records of their existence on the same spot at least since the fourteenth century. In the place of the oak at Guernica Isabel and Ferdinand, the first monarchs of united Spain, swore in 1476 to uphold the privileges of the Basques: and there too the Basque Parliament held its sessions, in a modest pavilion beside the tree.

The place of the oak miraculously survived the German bombing, but now there could hardly be a sadder place. The present oak sapling stands in a ceremonial enclosure, but it looks dusty and lifeless. The stone seats around it are permanently untenanted, the grass is unloved, the proud hopes of the Parliament House have decayed into dingy municipal deliberations. Over the oak tree there hangs, summer or winter, an air of failure: as if, having tried so hard for so many generations, the spirit of the place has lost heart.

Yet some magic lingers there. This is a site possessed by some penetrating quality of experience or emotion, and if you had never heard of the Basques, and knew nothing of the tree, or Basque history, or the bombing, still I think the place of the oak at Guernica would strike you as haunted. This is a sensation common in the Basque country. The Basques are not the best-looking people in Europe, and to my mind there is a certain balefulness to their landscapes, but mystery gives them a powerful fascination. The annals of the Basques are full of mystery—not merely the mystery of their origins, but eerie embellishments of legends and history too, devils and ghosts and arcane occurrences. In the spring the farmers of the Pyrenean foothills burn the bracken in their fields: and when at night you see the villages of the Basques illuminated from the slopes above by clumps of fire, blood-red smoke and a ghostly glow from the mountainside, you may be reminded of that queer heritage, and remember that no part of medieval Europe was more infested with witches.

The modern strangeness is largely age. The Basques have inhabited their country for a very long time indeed. Some scholars believe them to be the original inhabitants of the Iberian peninsula, squeezed over the century into this northern enclave. They were never conquered by the Moors who overran the rest of Spain, so that their blood remained unusually pure—they used to be considered the ultimate Spaniards, the gentry of gentry. Matters of pedigree have always been dear to them, and many a modest farmhouse in the hills brags an elaborate escutcheon above the door. Hundreds of thousands of aliens have migrated to the Basque provinces in the past half-century, but there is still an inbred feeling to the country: the extraordinary language, the romantic history, bind the people with a private subtlety. Basque architecture, too, gives a meshed flavour to the provinces. The old buildings are intricately half-timbered, and the new ones show a hereditary leaning towards the criss-crossed and the cantilevered, as though their designers would really like to fence them in with iron bars against the intrusion of outsiders.

Inside those houses, moreover, a mystic privacy often seems to reign. The Basques are not a gregarious Mediterranean people, though their genius often takes a hearty turn: theirs is a family society, based fundamentally upon isolated rural dwelling-houses. A Basque farm is thus a little world of its own. It is built to an Alpine pattern, and looks very like a Swiss chalet—living-rooms upstairs, working-rooms below, with the lush green grass sidling up to its front door, and the odd pyramidical haystacks of the Basques paraded down its meadows like troops of African dancers.

Every part of such a house seems to be full and active, and as the doors are opened for your inspection the members of the family are revealed as in some *tableau vivant*, each at work upon a speciality. In the kitchen, grandmother, all in black, is stirring a soup. In the work-shop, father is oiling a scythe. The daughter of the house is sewing in the living-room, surrounded by potted plants and oleographs: in a bedroom, the son is at his homework. And as the lady of the house places her hand upon the wooden latch of the last room of all, a distant secret look crosses her face—a madonna look, as in an old painting: a sweet smell of straw and warmth reaches you as the door creaks open, the light inside is dim, and there in the core of the farm-house you see the last members of its family: three stalwart rabbits, galloping in cages, two black and white cows, three little puppy-dogs gambolling at their leads, and a small grey donkey smiling from his manger.

Many other peoples live with their animals under the same roof: none that I know treat their beasts with quite the same collusive intimacy. It is as though the rabbits themselves speak Basque. Yet other aspects of the Basque mystique are anything but gentle. It is Basques, for instance, who have given the festival of San Fermin at Pamplona, in Navarre, its brutal excitement. There the bullfight, elevated else-where in Spain to a tragic ritual, is played as black farce: for enthusiastic amateurs are let loose in the streets before the bulls, and the festivities open with a harum-scarum chase to the bullring, the animals goaded and irritated into bewildered frenzy, the humans posturing and showing off, sprinting for dear life, standing their ground for moments of spectacular bravado or shinning ignominiously up trees. It is a display of coarse-grained appeal, and other Basque pastimes, too, are notable less for grace or delicacy than for brute primitivism.

There is, for instance, the trapping of the pigeons at Echalar. Every autumn thousands of pigeons pass through the Pyrenees on their way to warmer roosts, and a large proportion of them choose the easiest crossing of all at Echalar, where the pass is low and narrow. It is the traditional custom of the Basques to lie in wait for them there, and to drive them into nets by blowing bugles, beating drums, shouting and throwing white wooden disks about. There is the appalling sport called the goose-game, now mercifully almost extinct, in which a live goose is hung by its legs from a wire above the water, and men in boats try to decapitate it with their bare hands. There are innumerable contests of strength or appetite—log-chopping, beer-swilling, stone-cutting, steak-eating.

Most famous of all, there is *pelota*, a game which for the world at large sums up the reputation of the Basques. The Basques call it *jai-alai*—'the happy festival'—and this suggestively Japanesque title suits it, for it has a manner of violent sacrament not unlike *karate*. Everywhere in the Basque country, French or Spanish, the big pelota courts are prominent, like fives courts in every village: and wherever the Basques have gone they have taken the game with them, so that it has spread throughout Spain, is popular in Paris and thrives in Latin America. Nowhere can you see it more thrillingly played, or realize more vividly how close it lies to the roots of the Basque phenomenon, than in one of the great indoor courts of Bilbao, the metropolis of Basquerie.

There in the immense high-vaulted arena four young men in white bang a very hard ball against the three walls of the court. They do it with a queer hook-shaped basketwork glove, which gives them a sinister mutilated look, as though they have claws: and every time they hurl the ball out of this thing they do it with an immense physical exertion, a convulsion almost, straining every muscle, bent double with the effort, swinging the arm and its eerie hook with such momentum that when the ball leaves its socket at last—*whoosh*, it goes like a bullet, ricocheting madly here and there, off one wall, on to another, banging and bouncing and whistling and echoing—while the four young men hurl themselves, too, crazily across the court, with leaps and skids and tumbles, deftly catching the flying ball in their hooks and hurling it with paroxysms of determination back against the wall.

This is probably the most exhausting form of exercise man has ever devised. Even the spectators end a rally limp, and a professional pelota player is past his prime long before he is thirty. Throughout the performance half-a-dozen bookmakers, lined up beside the court in smart blue blazers, are shouting the odds at the tops of their voices, and gesticulating to customers on the balconied seats. If somebody upstairs signals that he wishes to place a bet, the bookie throws up a rubber ball with a hole in it: the client pushes his cash inside it and chucks it back again. This activity provides an odd embroidery to the tournament, and it is conducted with an enigmatic panache that is very Basque. It is as though the four lunatics on the court, convulsed with their daemonic zest, are being watched by an audience of shrewd and genial trusties from some less ferocious ward of the institution.

In Bilbao there are public pelota tournaments twice a day—one in the afternoon, one starting at 11 p.m. It is one of the more peculiar experiences of European travel to find this unique game proceeding with such tremendous vigour in the middle of the night, played by the only people in the world who really know how to do it.

For it is the fact of Basque survival, more perhaps even than the nature of Basqueness itself, that gives this country its curious enchantment. It is like seeing nature defied. All the odds of history, of politics, of ethnic development seem to be stacked against this strange enclave, and the clash between logic and emotion, between new conformity and ancient individuality, is disturbing and sometimes strangely beautiful to see. Off the road between Vittoria and Pamplona, in the heart of the Spanish Basque country, I drove up a track one day to eat a picnic lunch: and spreading out my cheese, wine and bread-hunks on the tawny grass, I caught sight of five or six little cypress trees, planted in formal gravity upon a nearby mound. Nothing could look more quintessentially Spanish than such a group of funereal trees, all alone there in that magnificent expanse, speaking as they did of order, propriety and sacred purpose.

Taking my glass with me, I wandered across to see why they had been planted there, expecting to find some holy shrine or Civil War memorial, embellished with the official ornaments of Madrid: but when I climbed to the top of their little mound, I found something very different in the hollow at my feet. It was a stone cromlech, a prehistoric cell or burial chamber, erected there by the distant progenitors of the Basques in the days when States had not been invented, Spain had not been named and Madrid did not exist. It looked rather toad-like—greyish, speckled with lichens, squat. Authority had fenced it with those cypresses as if to reduce it to a more familiar level, like a cemetery or a commemorative slab: but the wind whistled superbly through its great boulders, and made the line of little trees seem a finicky irrelevance.

CALCUTTA

Silently, silently trail the pickpockets, and sometimes a sleeper stirs in the arcades of Wellesley Place, raises an arm and returns to the catacomb. Everyone knows about Calcutta. Beneath the fairy lights of Howrah Bridge the rickshaws, the ravaged double-deckers, the bullock-carts and the Indians move world without end towards the railway station. Policemen with Lee-Enfields clamber from lorries, beggars without faces huddle against walls. The terrible attendants of the Hogg Market, brandishing their baskets, fall de-moniac upon the tourist taxis—'Everything open madam!' 'Here madam here!' 'Come this way! Come this way!'—their ingratiating frontal smiles curdling into loathing through the back window. Every-one knows about Calcutta. Everyone has seen its tall tenements stuffed with disease, its rioting millions in the battened streets, its children sprawled dead or alive on the midnight pavement. If there is one name that stands for misery, it is the name of this fearful and astonishing city—'Calcutta', as Mr. Eugene Fodor's guide expresses it, 'Vigorous, Vibrant, Versatile.'

I was looking for other images. I woke early and walked across Chowringhi into the green of the Maidan, before the sun rose and the heat-haze fell like a web upon us. It was lovely then in the park. Rooks cawed, kites hung, sparrows pecked, smiling pi-dogs padded by. Here and there across the grass white figures moved or loitered, and when-ever I paused I was sympathetically accosted. 'What you are seeing is the Theatre, built in honour of our great poet Rabindranath Tagore'. 'If I may say so you would be more comfortable where there are not so many ants'. 'Wouldn't you like a game of golf? I am teaching golf, you see: here are my golf clubs.'

I persevered, and finding myself unattended at last, sat on the grass and concentrated on the distant silhouette of the city to the north. Presently my prospect cleared, for I am psychic that way. The office blocks dissolved; the high rise buildings fell; the muddle resolved itself; and there I perceived in visionary outline the City of

Palaces—that first eager Calcutta, that landfall of modernity, which
the British built long ago upon the banks of the Hooghly. There were
the colonnades of Reason, there the elegant villas of Enlightened
Profit, garden by garden along Chowringhi. Storks dozed upon the
urns of Government House, and even as I sat there, out swept the
Governor-General in his equipage, with Her Excellency muslined
beneath her parasol—out through the great gate in billowing dust,
the lancers fluttering and clattering behind, while the passing coolies
dropped their loads to gape and salaam, and the redcoats presented
muskets.

It did not last, of course. Soon the heat arrived, and the noises of
the stirring city invaded the Maidan, and the pi-dogs pulled themselves together and started the day's long snarl. The professor of golf

Calcutta

had gone off to his office. I rose myself to leave; and there behind me, high on her throne upon an ornamental bridge, Queen Victoria herself sat slumped and accusatory in bronze. 'It is the Queen of England. She is the Queen Victoria. You want to change money? You want anything?'

Where are the box-wallahs? Silent the thickened voices in Spence's bar, absent the swaying Crimplene from the dance floor of the Grand. Gone is all that hierarchy of commerce, managing director to apprentice assistant, immortalized by the Calcutta memoirists—*Life and Ledger Beside the Hooghly*, or Montague Massey's classic *Recollections*, with a frontispiece of the Author in a high starched collar and a buttonhole, and many amusing anecdotes of life in the chummeries.

In the 1950s and 60s, that British business society still thrived, and one often saw its wives out shopping, or argued one's way laboriously into its presence when the front office clerk declined to honour one's travellers' cheque. It was a direct and living relic of the City of Palaces—itself a community of box-wallahs, in the days when the Honourable Company humbly received concessions from the Nawab of Bengal. The British businessman made Calcutta. It sprang from the loins of five-per-cent. There was nothing here before the Company came, but out of the dividendal urge arose the first and most terrifying of all monuments to the westernization of the East.

Go-downs, factories, counting-houses were the core of the city, and all around them the Bengalis swarmed in fascination—a few hundred in 1690, a few thousand in 1750, 800,000 by the 1890s, 3m. today. I love to wander around the city now and see, submerged but still visible, the structures of that old impetus; ramshackle warehouses, venerable banks; the long line of wharves, Garden Reach to Howrah, along which in all the old pictures lay the massed masts and smokestacks of the merchantmen; faded announcements of Victorian enterprise, saddlers and insurers and First Class Tailors, whose ornately-lettered signs stand wistfully faded among the cinema posters; even some stalwart survivors, ownership generally Indian but pedigree boldly British—Hamilton the Jewellers, Spences Hotel whose telegraphic address is *Homeliness*, *The Statesman* but not *The Englishman*, or that noblest patron of imperial reminiscence, Thacker, Spink the publishers.

The United Service Club is gone: but then it lost its point, did it not, when its committee overruled opposition to admit members of

50

Calcutta

the Bengal Pilot Service. They have pulled down the Bengal Club, once Macaulay's residence. For twenty years after Indian independence the British liked to say that the Calcutta commercial community was larger than it had ever been. Now, like a tissue finally rejecting a graft, Calcutta has rejected the box-wallahs: the chemistry of nationalism, taxation, trade unionism has forced them out at last, and the transplant of three centuries has just this minute ended.

'Does he, do you think', tactfully inquired the Bishop of Barrackpore, 'expect a T*I*P?' But no, my guide was not ready for one yet, having high hopes of further services to be performed, so I joined the Bishop on his verandah, where during a lull before evensong he was eating peanut butter sandwiches with a kind Anglican lady in blue. I was surprised to find him there, for European bishops are rare in Calcutta; but the Anglican rite, I gather, thrives, messed about of course by ecumenical irrelevancies and unnecessary reforms, but still recognizably the faith of Bishop ('Icy Mountains') Heber, who was Bishop of Calcutta in the 1820s, and thought the nearest terrestrial equivalent to Paradise to be the Government Botanical Gardens. Certainly the Bishop of Barrackpore was all an aficionado of the tradition could ask: cassocked, distinguished, fatherly, concerned about that T*I*P. Soon, he told me, he would be retiring. Going home? I wondered, but he answered in grave italics: 'Staying in India—*for ever.*'

The metropolitan cathedral of Calcutta is St. Paul's, one of the two great imperial initiatives to which the Governor-General Lord Auckland gave his approval, the other being the catastrophic invasion of Afghanistan. I went to a festival service there, and found it packed. Forty-eight electric fans, by my surreptitious count during the first lesson, whirled above us like divine helicopters; the officiating canon, copiously bearded and gorgeously coped, spoke the kind of Oxford English I imagine Jowett or Arnold to have spoken. We sang the hymn that says the Lord's throne shall never like earth's proud empires pass away. I wiped away a self-indulgent tear, as usual (for they are *always* singing that hymn in ex-imperial cathedrals): and as I left the cathedral a Balliol voice called kindly across the transept—'I say! Excuse me! You do know where we are, don't you, if you're coming to the children's dance drama in the parish hall?'

'*For ever*', the Bishop said, while the lady replaced the tea-caddy with a significant air: and pressing his point with unnecessary force, I thought, he showed me the picture of an eminent predecessor's

51

grave, high on a hill above Darjeeling—'Milman', he said, 'son of the Durham Milman, you know'.

They invited me to play the gubernatorial baby grand in the ballroom of Raj Bhavan—once the palace of the Viceroys of India, and modelled upon the Curzon family home at Kedleston in Derbyshire. There is no denying that this house has come down in the world, since Wellesley extravagantly began its construction in 1799—'India should be governed', it was said then, 'from a palace, not a counting-house, with the ideas of a Prince, not with those of a retail dealer in muslin. . . .' Reduced to the Governorate of Bengal when the capital was moved to Delhi in 1911, and to the Governorate of West Bengal after partition in 1947, its functions now rattle in it rather like a dehydrated pea in a juicy pod. The piano was badly out of tune, and seemed to want to play *Rustle of Spring*.

Still, the Indians have treated the building with respect, and showed it me most courteously. Calcutta is not, on the whole, vindictive about the Empire. Of course the lions, the unicorns and the imperial crowns have been prised away where priseable, but what remains is not abused. A king, three viceroys, a lieutenant-governor and an equestrian general still stand on their plinths in the Maidan: many more have been removed to retirement at Barrackpore, where they gaze sternly out of the garden shrubberies across the Hooghly river. They have not renamed Fort William, or Eden Gardens, or Hastings Square. They have not returned to the Burmese the pagoda which Lord Dalhousie looted from Prome in 1853. Nor have they toppled the weird column that commemorates good old David Octherlony, who was born in Massachusetts, whose thirteen Indian wives, they say, trundled about on thirteen elephants, and whose identity must be misty indeed to the passing Calcutta citizenry.

Among the most extraordinary sights in India is the stream of simple pilgrims that still flows awe-struck and amazed through the Victoria Memorial, that stately dome of white marble decreed by Lord Curzon to commemorate his monarch and himself. What are they thinking, these country families and groups of youths, as they pass from the Durbar Hall to Queen Mary's Room, and across to the Royal Gallery? Who can these bewhiskered magnates be, high and huge in their gilded frames? Why is the Female Aristocracy of Queen Victoria's Court perpetuated in massed lithography in the heart of Calcutta? Whose rheumy hand is this, thanking His Excellency for his condolences upon the death of the Prince Imperial? Reverentially they wander from hall to hall, gazing long at the ceiling mural portraying the prorogation of Parliament in July 1837, pondering deeply, as well they might, over the indescribable escritoire presented by King Edward in filial piety.

I would love to know what passes through their minds, and whose Raj they suppose this to have been. Sometimes they ask to see a picture in my guide book, as though it might elucidate a mystery, and they crowded around me in silent expectation when I sketched in my notebook the allegorical elevation across the east quadrangle: for there, looking past the central statue of the young Victoria, one sees perfectly aligned with her profile images of Lord Cornwallis and Sir Andrew Fraser, and Burne-Jones' great west window of St. Paul's—from the ear of the Queen, as it were, through the skulls of two satraps direct to the eye of God.

On a wall outside the Seth Sukhlall Karnani Hospital some verses are inscribed upon a plaque:

> *This day relenting God*
> *Hath placed within my hand*
> *A wondrous thing; and God*
> *Be praised at his command.*
>
> *Seeking His secret deeds*
> *With tears and toiling breath,*
> *I find thy cunning seeds*
> *O million-murdering Death.*

Here it was in 1898 that Surgeon-Major Ronald Ross, IMS, who was better at medicine than poetry, discovered the way mosquitoes spread malaria, one of the grand triumphs of the imperial experience.

> *I know this little thing,*
> *A myriad men will save,*
> *O death where is thy sting?*
> *Thy victory, O grave?*

Technique is what the British chiefly taught Calcutta. Profit brought them, faith blessed them, power kept them there and technique they left behind. System was their forte. School history books in India used to have a final chapter called Blessings of the English Raj. Exam papers always had questions about the Blessings, and

Calcutta

seventy years ago every conscientious Calcutta schoolboy, looking around him at the electric tramways and the General Post Office, or the High Court built to the pattern of Ypres Town Hall, could enumerate them pat: law and order, public health, irrigation works, schools, roads, bridges, railways and telegraphs.

High above the city now, to be seen equally from the roof of the Hindustan International Hotel or the squalidest canyon of Chitpur, the ugly steel lattice-work of the Howrah Bridge stands testimony to one kind of British technique: in a thousand grubby offices below the armies of bureaucracy, still consulting the precedents and cross-references of the Raj, bear inflexible witness to another. But the Blessings nowadays are harder to detect: they have not worn well in Calcutta, and are mostly corroded, or discredited, or buried in debris.

For this is like a city pursued by nightmares—chaos always at its heels, threats too hideous to contemplate and too shapeless to define. Technique itself has turned to anarchy, as though all the mechanism of modern urban life, grafted by the British in the days of the text-books, no longer recognizes authority: the trams, the telephones, the dustbin trucks, the big bridge, the policemen jumping from their lorry, the massed faces of a hundred million officials, the stopped clock, the Hogg Market attendants—all are jumbled, fused and disintegrated, while around the wreck of the system those dream figures revolve, corrupting the examiners or stabbing Congress supporters or pissing against the bakery wall.

And silently trail the pickpockets—silently after the Blessings, for when I was crossing Howrah Bridge in a rickshaw one night, a thief crept behind me with a very sharp knife, and while leaving my person fortunately intact, slit a hole in my bag and stole my wallet.

CAPRI

See that little blob, to the right of the olives there, scudding over a blue, blue sea with the dim line of Posilipo behind it, and a glitter of distant windows in Naples? That's the helicopter to Capri—ten minutes from the mainland to the windy promontory of Damecuta, high above the Blue Grotto. There it goes over the bay: Ischia on the horizon, Vesuvius to the north-east, and a faint clatter of its rotors now, as it approaches your cliff top. You can just make out its three passengers, cameras at the ready, and see the pilot's dark glasses behind his windscreen. It performs the journey six times each summer day: and every single passage that helicopter makes helps to bury a legend.

We need not discuss the undoubted fact that the little island of Capri, seventeen miles south of Naples, is the most beautiful place on earth. This has been universally recognized at least since the days of the Sirens, who had their choice of Homer's world and settled for these particular shores. Its waters so unbelievably blue, its gardens so sensually rich, its grottoes so romantic, its white villas set so delectably up hidden lanes, its smells so deliciously concocted of herbs, incense, roses, wines and earth, its red mullet so succulent, its spring flowers so heavenly, its air so magnificently clear, its rocks so properly savage—there is still nowhere quite like Capri, with its intoxicating sense of fertility, and its fields of prickly pear in the heat. Physically it remains incomparable, and makes almost all its rivals, from the Balearics to the Aegean, seem tawdry upstarts.

Most of us, though, have grown up with a particular vision of Capri—a vision compounded between the two wars, ennobled by some good writing, spiced with a suggestion of erotic goings-on, and given a gloss by the inclusion of Capri in the itinerary of every rich man's yacht, every celebrated divorcee's alimony, and every film star's winter publicity. This particular Capri, essentially an emanation of the '20s and '30s, is fading fast, in a world that is becoming too small for islands and too blasé for myths. Every day, every flight,

Capri

every travel agent's booking weakens the old voluptuous allure of Capri and makes the island, linked now with the mainland by every device of gregarious tourism, a little less extraordinary.

That helicopter hovers for a moment, fastidiously, and then descends upon an airport thronged with eager sightseers—children by the score, families on outings, even a solitary donkey, saddled up for visitors, meditating among the sage and marjoram. It settles there silently, rotors still, while its pilot prepares for the return journey: and there are not a few lovers of the old Capri, romantics, snobs, artists or mere traditionalists, who would not mind creeping up on it unawares and shoving it over the cliff.

Capri is a small steep island, nearly 2,000 feet high towards the middle, less than a mile wide at its neck, four miles long from cape to cape. Set so conveniently off the Sorrento peninsula, it might have been designed by Nature as a hideaway. The Emperor Augustus, indeed, saw its advantages so clearly that he went there to live and built himself a variety of villas, and if we are to believe Tacitus and Suetonius, his successor Tiberius had a high old time there in his senility, arranging moonlight orgies in sea caverns, hurling disagreeable acquaintances down bottomless precipices and generally behaving in the way most of us would, if we happened to be aged Roman emperors.

Then for several centuries this little Elysium was ignored by the world, mentioned only in the footnotes of the obscurer voyagers, and only half-heartedly threatened by Saracens and pirates. It was governed sometimes by the kings of Naples, sometimes by the rulers of Amalfi, sometimes by Normans, sometimes by Swabians, and for brief periods even by the British and the French. When the German travellers of the nineteenth century rediscovered the place, it was still pristine and primitive. Its peasant population fished, grew vegetables, made excellent wines and subsisted by a variety of happy crafts. The two little island villages, Capri and Anacapri, lived like toy towns among the vineyards, each with its church and its minute piazza, each cherishing a bitter and picturesque antipathy towards the other. The Capresi spoke a dialect all their own, mixed up with Greek words. They had a ruined monastery and a little harbour. They communicated with the mainland, as the Romans did, with simple hilltop semaphores, and sometimes even smoke signals.

This was the time of the grand romantics, when Rousseau's noble

Capri

savage had been neither discredited nor de-tribalized. Their heads a'swirl with Byronic rhythms, Rhineland visions and pantheistic yearnings, the Germans adored Capri. It became, for several generations of German tourists, the prime goal of southern travel—the eye of the sun, the crux of the Grand Tour. It was a German, in 1826, who first made famous the Blue Grotto—a marine cave, accessible only through a small hole in the cliff, whose astonishing phenomena of refraction so enraptured visitors that in no time at all lesser grottoes were being re-christened all over the island—the Green Grotto, the White Grotto, the Red Grotto, even the Obscure Grotto. Throughout the nineteenth century, if you thought of Capri, you thought of grottoes: also sunshine, young wine, Germans and Tiberius.

Thus was founded the modern legend of Capri, but it reached its heady climax after the First World War, when the island became, above all else, a place of voluntary exile for hedonists. They were not all rich hedonists. Somerset Maugham tells a cautionary tale about an English bank clerk who, coming into a twenty-five year annuity, gives everything up and goes to live on Capri. Living the lotus-life happily enough until the money dries up, he subsides into degraded poverty, and we leave him dying destitute and half-crazed on a hillside. Much wealth did, however, settle upon the island—and much hauteur, too. Umberto II of Italy loved the place, and regularly moved there with his entire court. Queen Victoria of Sweden was a frequent visitor. The English aristocracy adopted the island, the grand white yachts of Empire lay frequently off the little harbour and one indomitable peer, for a substantial wager, walked stark naked from Capri to Anacapri. Capri was essentially a residential resort, a place to spend the winter in, or live the whole year round. Many habitués had two houses indeed, within the 3,000-odd acres of that opulent rock—one facing north, for the summer, the other with its back to the winter winds.

And to capture this transient scene, to immortalize it as few pleasure havens have ever been saved from oblivion, a whole pack of writers fell upon the island—attended, as always, by those miscellaneous originals, charlatans and dilettantes who cling to the coat-tails of art. Norman Douglas' masterpiece *South Wind* is all about Capri, and so are two of Compton Mackenzie's best books. D. H. Lawrence wrote a story about Capri, the Italian poetess Ada Negri celebrated the island in a famous cycle of poems. Axel Munthe told

Capri

the semi-fictional story of his love affair with the place to such effect that *The Story of San Michele* has been translated into almost every literary language, and still sells bravely in paperback after thirty-five years of success. Some 600 books are said to have been written about Capri, at one time or another, and the island was honoured in the heyday of Impressionism by a serenade from Claude Debussy.

Overlapping the villa life of the rich, a flourishing café society developed, and the little piazza of Capri, scarcely bigger than a large salon, became one of those half-dozen places on earth where, if you sat long enough, you could expect to see all the famous walk by. Attracted by the presence of Norman Douglas, a notorious but kindly pederast, sexual non-conformists of all kinds made the place their headquarters, and *la dolce vita* flourished among the rose gardens. Amiable eccentrics of many tastes postured the years away at the Gran Caffè, and now and then there arose among the foreign community one of those bitter antagonisms, clique against clique, that so often give tang to the artificial existence of idle expatriates.

It was, in short, for those few of that dead world able to enjoy it, a proper little paradise: boats were infrequent, trippers were rare, the proletariat of Naples were subtly encouraged to go to Ischia instead, and probably nowhere in Europe felt cosier, warmer, more intimate and more fun than a table in the sun in that fortunate piazza. But it went the way of the dodo—by the pressures of historic evolution. Cast your eye to the right, now, and you will see something foaming and white scudding across the bay. It is the *aliscafo* from Naples, a hydrofoil that does the trip in half an hour with a truly magnificent panache. Down in the harbour below you, between a grey gunboat and a yacht, lies the morning *vaporetto* from the mainland, still hazy about the funnel. And here flooding into the piazza, pouring out of taxis, out of buses, out of horse carriages, out of the steep funicular that runs up from the waterfront—wearing floppy straw hats and rope-soled shoes and pink jeans and multifarious bangles—festooned with cameras, inquiring the price of swimsuits, unfolding maps, touching up their lipstick beneath the campanile—talking German, English, French and every regional variety of Italian—young and old, blatant and demure, strait-laced and outrageous, earnest and frivolous and thrilled and sick-to-death-of-it-all—here past the café tables streams the first quota of the morning's tourists, who may number, on an average summer day in the 1970s, anything up to 4,000 at a go.

Capri

So another Capri has evolved, to meet the exigencies of an age in which seventeen miles of water scarcely counts as wet. There is still a small foreign community on the island. There are still a few artists, here and there, and sometimes a visiting writer pokes his way about those old haunts of the story-tellers. Capri has geared itself, though, to the requirements of mass travel, and in particular of the package tour, in which nothing is left to whim. A motor road connects Capri and Anacapri, their old feuds long since buried, and along it the taxis and open-roofed buses roar with a perpetual blasting of horns and showy changing of gears. They have even built a highway down to the Blue Grotto, half of whose point used to be that you could go there only in a boat, with a colourful Capri fisherman, wearing a striped shirt and no shoes, to row you there in a cloud of anecdote. The shopkeepers of the two villages, once so modest and unobtrusive, have learned the technique of pounce and ingratiation—'*No need to buy! No need to buy! Come inside and see my little shop!*' Prices have reached, and even surpassed, the classically ruinous standards of Venice herself. So few Capresi bother to go to sea any more that most of the fish is imported from Naples with the tourists, and half the wine sold behind a Caprese label comes in fact from the mainland. There is a chairlift to the summit of Mount Solaro, the highest point in the island, and a shop near the piazza at Capri where you may have your eyelashes dyed.

The old hands loathe it all. They badly miss the stylish old days, and sometimes wish King Umberto were back on the throne of Italy. Capri, they say, is theirs no longer: the tourist agencies have usurped the island, and all is vulgar mechanics. Scores of villas have been turned into pensions. Almost every month some well-known foreign resident leaves for home, with tears and hugs in the piazza, and an agitated jangling of bracelets. Capri rarely appears nowadays in the repertoires of the novelists. Outclassed by St. Tropez, Marbella and points east, its name is no longer a prurient word, and even the tales of old Tiberius are being systematically debunked. Mediterraneanism, as Nietzsche dubbed the southern movement of European art, has shifted its focus eastward, to Greece, Turkey and the Aegean. No electronic Debussy now finds his inspiration here. The Blue Grotto probably hasn't been painted for years. Norman Douglas lies beneath the cypresses in the cemetery.

So it seems at first—perfection *passé*. The peasants of Capri, though,

Capri

have been so miraculously enriched that less than twenty miles from the blotched miseries of Naples there are virtually no poor; the average working man feels no regrets; and the casual visitor, too, if he has a day or two to spare and kick his heels, may find that if the old Capri is almost dead, the new one can still be halfway to most people's idea of Heaven.

For there remains a compulsive allure to this minute but infinitely famous place. The very first person I saw in the piazza of Capri, when I arrived there for the first time in my life, was the late Randolph Churchill, hunched over a Cinzano, among the London papers, lost in the enthralment of electoral prospects. I was not surprised to see him there, for somehow Capri retains a stature beyond its size, and if you spend half an hour in the piazza in the spring, before the summer crowds destroy its intense and toylike charm, you may still feel yourself to be sitting in one of the special places of the world.

Here comes Hans Spiedel, a cheerful deaf-mute, once a well-known ballet dancer in Austria, now queerly slung about with amulets and satchels and roaming the piazza like an elfin sage. There is Baron Cottrau, who keeps an antique shop along the road, and presides over a circle of admirers at a corner table of the Gran Caffè. There goes the Countess Bismarck, and there is Lady Archibald, and there is Gracie Fields, and there the American plutocrat who made his pile with cat food. Elderly ladies in corduroy scarves, bead necklaces and a great deal of rouge embrace each other noisily among the waiters. A priest in a shovel hat walks purposefully out of one alley and into another. Three exquisite young Neapolitans, looking like dissolute Bourbon princes, lounge catlike over their coffees, watching the girls go by. Outside the little police station a solitary gendarme gravely stands, and at her balcony beside the bell tower the bored operator at the public telephone office, short of customers, leans on the parapet and does her nails. There are silks in one little shop, straw hats in another, flowers in pots around the corner, newspapers from half Europe, cheeses on strings and meat on hooks in the shadow of the passage-way to the funicular. And through it all, with shopping baskets and fine broad shoulders, the ordinary Capresi bustle about their business—still, for all the corrosions of easy money and celebrity, a surprisingly sweet and simple people. They give to the island, even now, an underlying sense of pagan innocence—the same folk-setting against which, down the centuries, the pleasures of despots and sybarites must always have blazed with such crimson emphasis.

Capri

Capri is still a place where you may take long solitary walks in scented sunshine, where cows are still to be found pensive in lonely sheds on cliff tops, where flowers are everywhere, and gentle people, where geckos flicker and cocks crow, where the cabman will proudly show you his brand new barouche, tailor-made on the mainland, where medieval alleyways are still crooked and suggestive, and country lanes go meandering around the villas, through the prickly pears and the wisteria, over a ridge and around a vineyard, beyond the great rocks of the Faraglioni, where the rare blue lizards of Capri live, until at last you are deposited, breathless and elated, upon that magnificent high promontory, looking over to Sorrento, where Tiberius built the most spectacular of his palaces, and threw several of his more irritating supplicants headlong into the Tyrrhenian Sea.

Capri is ruined, say those who knew it in another era, and anyway Tiberius never did anything of the sort: but for those who visit the island for the first time today, and can cock an ear beyond the motor horns and the tourist patter, it still offers distinct and delectable echoes of its Siren song. And here is a personal confession: for my own tastes, one of the most exciting experiences in Europe today is to land on Capri in the helicopter, sweeping in so debonair over that miraculous blue sea, whirring gently into the sage and emerging from the aircraft, warmth and freshness all about you, to find yourself face to face with that donkey.

CHICAGO

Two remarkable sculptures embellish Chicago, Illinois. Both are by great masters from abroad, both stand grandiosely alfresco, and each represents, no doubt unintentionally, a Chicago attitude—a motive in the life of the city.

The first is by Picasso, and it stands unavoidably in the middle of Civic Center Plaza, itself the heart of downtown Chicago. This artifact is very tall, is made of steel, and looks like different things to different Chicagoans—to some a horse, to some a bird, to clots a load of old junk, to sophisticates *nothing*, my dear fellow, just *nothing*, merely an expression of the creative act. To everybody, however, it represents one aspiration: cultured urbanity, a condition towards which Chicago has been assiduously striving throughout its brief but blistered history.

The second sculpture is by Henry Moore, and it stands less ostentatiously on the outskirts of the city, in the campus of the University of Chicago. This one is squat, bronze and burly. It is an alarming bulbous object like an egg, or a helmet, or a huge bald head, and it seems to heave itself out of the ground organically, beside a tennis court. It is called Nuclear Energy, and it stands near the spot where Enrico Fermi and his colleagues achieved the first atomic chain reaction: but in the Chicago context it stands for everything hefty, violent and swaggering in the traditions of the city, gunfight and cattle-yard, railroad king and ethnic fury.

The two great pieces have never stood face to face, but the aspects of Chicago which they seem to symbolize are always clashing, mingling or standing aghast at each other: and it is the co-existence of two such persistent strains, each in some ways slightly comic, but each magnified by history or environment into an immense social force, which makes Chicago one of the most perpetually surprising cities in the world.

The lady who presides over the observation floor of the Board of

Chicago

Trade building generally prefers to look north, I think, in the general direction of the Picasso. She gives you a map, indeed, and offers a brief but telling statistic about railroad stations, but she talks most eloquently about the uptown view, where the glittering apartment blocks gaze superbly across Lake Michigan, like heirs-apparent to the brownstones at their feet.

From the start Chicagoans were eager to prove that they could be just as cultivated, just as sensitive, as any patriotic Easterner or European. They built their mansions, financed by the enormous profits of railroad and prairie, with an orgiastic flourish—château or mock-Tudor, oak-beamed or castellated, hung about with the most expensive pictures and draped in unobtainable tapestries. They did not want to appear hicks. Oscar Wilde, in his most preposterously haestetic period, was kindly received by Chicago society, on account of his being a famous writer, and huge museums were presently crammed with loot from the older civilizations, enabling over-educated daughters to swell parental hearts by recognizing a Botticelli when they saw one.

This old snobbism was, of course, partly just social affectation. It survives even now, and still looks pretty silly. Nowhere in the world, I swear, will you hear the word 'Society', with a capital S, used so frequently: and nowhere is Society more fun to watch—eating an ineffably English tea, perhaps, in a carriage-trade Chicago restaurant, with Jasmine Tea and Toasted Muffins beside the indoor goldfish pool, overhung by chandeliers and baskets of artificial sweet peas, served by satiny capped-and-aproned waitresses.

It looks like a vanished Europe queerly mutated, as if by some malfunctioning time machine. It has a sprayed, clamped look. Its children behave with an almost fictional decorum. Its daughters wear pearls. Its young mums look as though they have come direct from committee meetings of charitable balls. Its husbands look as though they keep fit by riding hunters through parks before breakfast. Its grandmothers, best of all, talk in throaty turtle voices, as though the words are being squeezed out from beneath the carapace: and they are heavily loaded with inherited gewgaws, and are inclined to call the waitress 'Child', as though expecting pretty curtseys in return. 'Would you care for some more Jasmine Tea, Mrs. Windlesham? Do you desire another Toasted English Muffin?' 'Why thank you, child —how pretty you are looking today!' 'Thank *you*, Mrs. Windlesham, it's always a pleasure to serve you and the members of your family.'

Chicago

But if Chicago's yearning for tradition and urbanity is sometimes ridiculous, in other ways it is noble. It is not only a search for class, it is a hunger too for splendour. Thanks partly to the pretensions of the Mrs. Windleshams, trying so hard to keep up with the Cabots or the Cecils, this is a city of majestic presence. Consider the view on a spring morning, for instance, from the shore of the Lake beside the Planetarium. A belt of green parkland fills the foreground, plonked about by tennis balls, splashed with tulips and cherry blossoms; then a moving strip of traffic, streaming relentlessly along the expressway; then, beyond the sunken railroad tracks, the tight-packed façade of Lake Shore Drive, which reminds me of Prince's Street in Edinburgh. Above and behind all this rises the skyline of downtown Chicago, and there it all comes true. It is one of the grandest of all silhouettes. It is a glorious jumble of styles and conceptions—here a cylinder, there a pyramid, Gothic bobbles and Victorian scrolls, bumps, domes, cubes, towers like the lattice masts of old battleships, gables, even a steeple—a tremendous congeries of buildings, without balance or symmetry, which properly suggests a metropolis thrown together in an enormous hurry by a race of unappeasable giants.

Chicago fostered a famous literary school in the 1930s. Its wealth and earnestness have attracted men of talent and learning from all over the world. It seems to have a university, museum or art gallery in every other street, and even the *Encyclopædia Britannica* emigrated here long ago (leaving the more determined Anglophiles and patriots, like me, still firmly consulting our eleventh Edition, 1910). But its real splendour lies in its architecture. It is one of the great architectural showplaces of the world, and long since offered its own retort to the judgement passed by Oscar Wilde, wearing knee-breeches and a buffalo robe during a Press conference at the Grand Pacific Hotel: 'Your city looks positively too dreary to me.'

For whatever other criticisms may be thrown at Chicago, positively too dreary it does not look. It is full of masterpieces. The skyscraper was born in Chicago. Frank Lloyd Wright was a Chicago architect, and when Hitler closed the Bauhaus, Ludwig Mies van der Rohe made Chicago the world capital of architectural modernism. Mies, as every Chicago sophisticate likes to remember him, was the Michelangelo or Christopher Wren of this city. He lived there, in one of his own apartment blocks, and the city is stamped all over with his genius: a chill but towering genius of cube, glass and right-angle, which pre-shadowed the age of the rockets and the computers, and

Chicago

will always make Chicago as symbolic of the 1950s and 1960s as
Florence is emblematic of the Renaissance.

With Mies van der Rohe Chicago has finally made it. That great
collection of buildings beyond the expressway, crowned by his dis-
passionate vision, vindicates all the old pretensions of this city—
reaching as it did, for so many generations, so ludicrously but so
poignantly for style.

Size, push and power come more easily to Chicago. 'Sir,' a nineteenth-
century visitor was told by the conductor, as his train ran into Union
Station, 'you are approaching the boss city of the universe!' Chicago
still has a beefy reputation, and a boisterous penchant for superlatives
—Biggest, Best, Richest, Heaviest. Brawn and blarney remain
essential to the Chicago atmosphere, particularly well reflected I
think in the menu of the Café Bohemia, which offers haunches of
lion, beaver, moose, jaguar and many other fauna—'Lion steaks are
real good,' they told me there, 'tiger too, tiger's delicious when it's
on'. 'I Will' is the unofficial slogan of Chicago: or 'I Will', as the
columnist Max Royko once suggested, 'If I Don't Get Caught'.

For that glorious waterfront is thin. It is like the front of some
colossal folly. Immediately behind it sprawls the tumultuous Loop,
the business district, still enclosed more or less by the clanking
loop of the Elevated Railroad, and instinct with memories of bur-
lesque, gangland and political machine. And behind the Loop again
extend the neighbourhoods, the vast hinterland of this metropolis,
the Negro quarters, the dingy tenements of the poor whites, half-
cleared slum and railway track, steel mill and used car lot—Lawndale,
Woodland, Oakland, Halsted Street and Blue Island, where the
Ukrainians, the Lithuanians, the Mexicans, the Poles and the Sicilians
fitfully preserve their tastes and customs, in the wasteland of their
new world.

This is Capone's Chicago, beer-ringed, smoke-filled, whisky-
breathed, a powerful, dangerous and notorious place. Almost nothing
about it is small. Its area is vast. Its energy is tireless. Its problems are
tremendous problems—Race, Poverty, Violence. Its solutions are
grand solutions—immense slum-clearances, huge new roads, gigantic
universities. It is full of crime and corruption, but it does not feel,
like Manhattan, locked within its own anxieties, congested by traffic
and exhausted by argument. This is the Windy City, and gusts of
lake and prairie bluster incessantly down these streets, never scouring

68

Chimera

them indeed, but keeping all their rubbish helter-skelter on the move.

Chicago is never *tired*. Here one still senses the insatiable optimism of the Victorians. This remains a city of the railway age, with all its swollen faults and merits. 'Purr-fect Transport', proclaims a poster for the Baltimore and Ohio, and the railroad tracks still flood into this city like so many rivers, each to its towered or colonnaded terminus. Here in the birthplace of nuclear power you may still hear the mournful clang of the locomotive bell, as the freight train edges its way through the downtown streets, and here the old El, so long banished from most American cities, still sways merrily around the Loop, its cars jutting so perilously over the curves that it looks like a toy train in a nursery, approaching its inevitable derailment. Chicago has a Pullman braggadocio—swagger of brass and green liveries, swank of cheroot, wink of deal or shady profit.

It is an elemental sort of strength. One seems to feel the energies of America pouring into this heartland city, to be processed, refined or coagulated. The Chicago Stockyards are no longer the grisly spectacle they used to be, for nowadays most of the cattle are slaughtered at source, but among their maze of cattle-pens, all the same, you still know yourself to be in the capital of the beef country. The yards still smell strongly of manure and hot animal, and sometimes offer, obliquely perhaps through a cattle-pen gap, classic cameos of western life: the steers slithering frenzied by, breathing heavily, gasping, with a thud of hoofs in the mud and straw—and behind them out of sight the cowhands, cracking their whips and yippying—and then one glimpses their Stetsons, bobbing above the barricades, and one hears their swearing and spitting and coughing—and then for a moment they too appear in your gap, a couple of brown unshaven men, whose expressionless blue eyes look out at you with a haunting detachment, as though they have never emerged from those stock-yards in all their lives, but will die inside there with their whips in their hands.

Chicago is a brutal city. It always has been, and used to be rather proud of the fact. Tourists were taken to see the site of the St. Valentine's Day massacre, until a Canadian bought the celebrated garage wall for re-erection in his garden. Extortion and gang rivalry still happen in Chicago, but nowadays violence feeds upon different and deeper passions too—passions of race or ideology. One cannot spend long in Chicago today without sensing the under-currents of fear and resentment which swirl beneath the great city. The Chicago

Chicago

police cars move about with weird and ominous bleeping noises: and it is as though they are keeping an electronic eye upon every emotion of the place, love or hate or nostalgia or avarice, for computer-stacking at headquarters.

'Lucky you got me', the cab-driver nearly always seems to say, if you want to visit the neighbourhoods. 'Not many guys would take you. I tell ya, I was a Marine four years, I fought in eight major battles, eight *major* battles, and believe me if any of these blacks gets in my way I'll just run 'em down, just like that. Lock your door now. Like I say, it's lucky you found me. Not many guys would come out this way.'

One such reassuring veteran took me to a street corner in Lawndale, a toughish Negro neighbourhood, which is almost a shrine of Chicago's unhappy preoccupations. It is called the Wall of Respect, and it is painted all over with frescoes commemorating the Negro struggle for power or self-respect: portraits of martyrs, emblems of epic sacrifice, symbolic scenes of hope or grievance, bitter jokes, exhortations, big Guernica-like pictures of tragedy. 'There's more inside', a passing youth told me, and sure enough in the bar across the way, roped off inside its dark recess like a wall-painting in a cave, there faintly glowed a huge wall-collage of clippings, paintings and photographs, which reminded me of those side-chapels full of relics, ex votos and discarded crutches that one sees in the side-chapels of Spanish cathedrals.

It disturbed me, as though I had stumbled upon some secret consecration of the city, an inner dynamism. I felt I was intruding upon private quarrels. Outside in the street the cab-driver was pointedly reading a paper-back: inside the bar the Negroes did not look at me, but leant at the bar laughing over private jokes, answering my diffident inquiries only in a kind of amused ellipse.

Sometimes the twin strains of Chicago, the colossal and the cultivated, are blended in a scene or an institution. This produces a flavour altogether unique to this city—which is, of course, a great capital without a nation, a Vienna that never had an Empire. It is, I think, essentially a saltless flavour—bland, fleshy perhaps. One misses intellectual Jews in this city, or sardonic Yankees. The wide pale lake, though it has its perilous gales, its ships direct from Europe, even its modest tides, is distinctly not the open sea, but looks as though its water would be soft and slithery to the touch. The bluster-

Chicago

ing winds carry no tang, the waterfront spray leaves no tingle on the face. The posh apartment blocks on the Edgewater shore, complete with their marinas, striped umbrellas and private beaches, are like segments of Beirut deposited upon the edge of the Caspian. The conversation of Chicago mostly lacks edge, and tends towards the exhortatory monologue.

In the same way the uniquely Chicago phenomena are less stirring than stunning. They bowl you over by scale, or momentum. Take for instance the commodity market on the ground floor of the Board of Trade building. This is a peculiar spectacle. The setting is a large hall in which are sunk a number of pits like arenas for cockfights, or rings for Persian wrestling. Standing in these bowls are several hundred men behaving in a very eccentric way—holding up their forefingers in stylized gestures, suddenly jerked into activity by invisible alarms, shouting, lapsing into morose introspection, apparently bursting into song, and generally carrying on so incomprehensibly that the sensible females looking on from the public gallery are left in a state of distracted disbelief. Really, one seems to hear them say, grown men, behaving like a lot of clowns. This is Chicago, though, and behind the lunacy lies power, wealth and earthiness. Look to your left, and there you will see upon the notice-boards the names of the commodities handled in this internationally significant exchange: soybean, corn, oats, sorghum, pork bellies—substances which bring you instantly back to reality, place the antics below in a new and less comical perspective, and remind you once more of Chicago's organic kind of power.

Not far away is Playboy Mansion, the sybaritic palace-pad of Hugh Hefner the publisher. I have never penetrated this building, which looks rather like a Soviet Embassy in one of the lesser European capitals, and is similarly unenticing to gate-crashers: but for my purposes it does not matter, for the point of Playboy Mansion is not the fact but the legend. In this it honours a tradition of the Chicago tycoons, who often grew celebrated upon rumour—mouth-to-mouth statistics, tall tales of unimaginable opulence, whispers of enviable excess. Chicagoans, by and large, seem very proud of Playboy Mansion, and willingly take you to peer wanly, like displaced persons, through its high railings. It is not merely that dozens of sexy girls are said to live in there, or that the kitchen is staffed by twelve chefs around the clock, or that you can swim out of the swimming-pool into a subterranean grotto, or even that the whole building forms a

Chicago

controlled environment, where Mr. Hefner can decree the coming of night and day, or the shift of the seasons. All this represents, of course, the epitome of Chicago's instinct for scale and technique, but there is more to the legend of Playboy Mansion than mere tycoonery. There is the intoxicating knowledge that real Poets, Writers, Actors and Artists frequent that house, that even now Mr. Hefner is probably hard at work upon his Philosophy, attended by deft-shuffling library Bunnies—that besides being terrifically rich, gaudy, vulgar, spectacular and big, Playboy Mansion is genuinely and avant-gardedly *cultured*!

For a last illustration of this particular Chicago sensation—which strikes me as the feeling of Rubens, as against the feeling of Rembrandt—let us stand after dinner on a wet, blustery, overcast night upon the bridge that crosses the Chicago River beside Tribune Tower. We shall see one of the great urban vistas of the world, finer than anything in Manhattan, but our hearts somehow will not soar. We shall merely be stopped in our tracks with wonder. In the foreground, on the left, the ornate old Wrigley Building stands savagely floodlit, a vast slab of white, but beyond it in relative darkness the tree-lined North Michigan Avenue—'The Magnificent Mile'—extends urbanely to the north. Thus through alternating dazzle and shadow we peer towards the other end, and there in a theatrical refulgence of lights stands a monumental group of structures, one against the other in deep projection.

Ironically in the centre of the group is the quaint old Chicago water-tower—Wilde's 'castellated monstrosity with pepper boxes stuck all over it'—brilliantly illuminated and looking from this distance like some kind of sacred totem. Behind, around and above it stand hotels and tall office blocks, plunged in darkness or ablaze with light, and loomed over tremendously by the black shape of the John Hancock Building, the second tallest in the world, a building clamped together with diagonal steel struts, like Prometheus chained. Up this vast tapering form one's eye rises, until the summit of the building is lost in swirling cloud: and somewhere up there through the drizzle a beacon searchlight plays, diffused mysteriously on the overcast, flashing off steel faces or slabs of glass. So low is the cloud, so tossed about by the winds, so dramatically illuminated by that restless beam, that once more the image seems to be of the steam age, and Chicago in its most formidably modern quarter harks back again to the flicker of furnaces in the night.

Chicago

But salt, no, only limitless power: and when the daylight comes, and those immense structures fall back into their respective identities, out of the half-dream of their midnight ensemble, some of the magic fades, the water-tower is only a disused municipal facility after all, and most of the buildings turn out to be rather ordinary.

This is the most pungent surprise of Chicago—its underlying homeliness. I use the word in its English sense, to mean domesticity, unpretending kindliness, but even so I am aware it will infuriate Chicagoans. Almost any conclusion about their city infuriates Chicagoans. Theirs is one of the most perilous of all cities to write about, for they have a fatal gift of putting the most sympathetic visitor on the offensive. Whenever I go to the place it seems to be rumbling still with resentment against some recent essay: on my first visit it was a *New Yorker* piece by A. J. Liebling that the city was regurgitating, on my last a book by Norman Mailer. You cannot please Chicago.

But there we are: Chicago strikes me as essentially a nice, ordinary, middling, homely sort of town. People write affectionate songs about it—'My kind of town, Chicago is'—'Chicago, Chicago, that wonderful town'—not merely because of its euphonious Indian name, but also because it is somehow graspable and human. It never feels like megalopolis. For all its vicious reputation, for all its force and wealth, it still manages to feel like a provincial city in an older America. Every night the Negro migrants step off the midnight train from the South, as they have since the end of the Civil War, and in the streets of the Loop you may often see, dressed up in touching finery for a day in the big city, country corn-folk window-shopping, resisting Junior's demand for a complete circuit of the El, or sucking ice-creams beside the Picasso. On the lake shore one hot afternoon, passing through a bronzed Chicago family sporting themselves Americanly on the sward, with space-rays and Japanese cameras, I came across the patriarch of the group, an aged Lithuanian, ruminating behind white walrus moustaches in the tinted-glass recesses of the family car—a true image of the American idea.

People are polite in Chicago, when they are not rioting or expressing the darker prejudices. The pace is not quite so fast as it is in Los Angeles or New York, and the citizen is not so soured. He takes time to tell you the way, concludes with a pleasantry, very likely asks you where you are from or tells you about the eight major battles of his

Chicago

military career. 'Thank you', said I to the waitress at Marshall Field's, when she brought me my English Muffins. 'Enjoy them', she sweetly replied, as though she had made them herself from Grandma's recipe. 'All of CAR', says a sign at a parking lot in the Loop, in my favourite Chicago declaration, 'must be in off of sidewalk before getting Ticket'.

Of course this is Norman Rockwell's America. Chicago really is, in a newly significant sense, the All American capital. It remains relatively immune to the cosmopolitan forces, the last great stronghold of American Values. Here the charm of a lost America survives, in patriotic sentiments, family lakeshore groups, rhodomontade and nightly servings of what used to be called Showbiz. Parochial pride is endearingly intense: there is a mysterious channel on Chicago TV, never explained to me, which seems to transmit absolutely nothing except very slow-moving publicity films about the city itself. 'What are you?' asked the elevator man at the Merchandise Mart one day, eyeing my Chelsea haircut with an All-American eye, 'some kind of a singer?'

I can see that many young Americans must regard the place as Nadirville, a very sump of all they most detest about the American Way of Life: but I love it all, in a nostalgic, detached sort of way, knowing that I shall presently be taking the aircraft back to New York and dear old decadent London. Chicagoans, of course, will think me patronizing, but I do not mean it so. For me the persistent provincialism of Chicago makes perfect sense. Urbanity comes easy nowadays, power is painfully old hat, nobody wants to live in Megalopolis. The small nations are coming into their own, as the happiest environment for human existence, and so too are the provincial cities, where plainer human values can survive, where time is a little less compressed and there is space for a few extra prepositions, as you manoeuvre the CAR in off of the sidewalk.

And of these cities Chicago is the boss.

CEYLON

At my window, a shiny-feathered crow; outside, an elderly steam locomotive sporadically snorting; palm trees in the yard, a glimpse of sea, the beginning of a heat haze, four or five distant swathed figures foraging upon the beach. The old electric fan above my head creaked protestingly every third time round. The servant who brought my breakfast shuffled comfortably about in sandals and called me 'Master'. There was a smell of eggs and bacon from below. I was awakening to a morning in Ceylon, from whose medieval name, Serendib, Horace Walpole derived the abstract noun *serendipity*—the faculty, as the *Oxford Dictionary* has it, 'of making happy and unexpected discoveries by accident'.

Not every Ceylonese discovery is happy, for this is an island that has seen better days, and has lately been depressed by addled politics and false finance. Unexpected, though, Ceylon certainly is—a fascinating anomaly of the Indian Ocean, a humped oval island not far north of the equator, with some of the most exquisite scenery in the world and a mountain so holy, to devotees of several religions, that even the agnostic butterflies hazily meander there, when they feel the death-urge coming on.

Northern Ceylon is actually joined to southern India by a chain of sandy reefs called Adam's Bridge, yet the two countries scarcely feel in the same continent. Ceylon is plump, genial, richly vegetated. Ceylon is small—two-thirds the size of Ireland, with ten-and-a-half million people. Ceylon has always given pleasure: to the ancient Indians it was Lanka, the Resplendent Land, to the Moors the Isle of Delight, to the Chinese the Jewelled Island, to the Victorians the Pearl of the Indian Ocean, and even the sensible Dutch thought the shape of the place reminiscent of a dressed ham hanging from the rafters. Spices, rubies, beautiful slaves, aromatic teas have been staples of Ceylon down the centuries. A gently festive air seems to linger over the island, whatever the excesses of its politicians, and leaves in almost every visitor's mind an impression of balanced serenity.

In fact the island's history has been distinctly rumpled. The Hindu epics peopled Ceylon ferociously with demon-kings and monkey-armies, and in recorded times Indians, Portuguese, Dutchmen and Britons have all invaded the island, with varying degrees of penetration—until the British deposed it by force in 1815 there was still an independent dynasty of kings in the valleys of the interior. Hundreds of thousands of Indian Tamils have crossed the narrow strait to settle in Ceylon, and the island races have been so piquantly compounded that when I recently looked up the directors of a Ceylonese firm called Tuckers Ltd., I discovered that their names included Kotswala, Aloysius, Fernando and Mrs. Mavis Tucker herself. Catholicism has been strong since the first European conquests, Hinduism thrives among the Tamils, and the clash and flare of the devil-dancers still enlivens the street corners of the island, and comforts its timorous villagers.

It is Buddhism, though, which sets the calm tone of Ceylon, and so differentiates it from the frenzied peninsula to the north. Buddhism came to the island from India in the third century B.C., when the Ceylonese king, Tissa, was converted by a missionary from India. The sweet legends of the faith infuse the place now, its great ruined cities still meditate in the jungles, and its gentleness still makes the start of a Ceylonese day, whatever the newspaper headlines are screaming, a pleasant prod to one's serendipity. The waiter put down my breakfast that morning, and said he hoped I would have an enjoyable day. I told him I was going to make a pilgrimage to the grave of my father-in-law, a planter who had died in Ceylon during the war.

'By God', he said at once, 'that's good, that's very good—parents is a bigger thing than the Lord Buddha himself': and picking up my shoes, to clean them for the occasion, he bowed gracefully and withdrew.

On an artificial lake in the middle of the island, surrounded by soft wooded hills, stands the small city of Kandy, last capital of the Ceylonese kings, and still the home of all that is most deeply indigenous to Ceylon. The Dutch and the Portuguese never subdued this ancient place, and the British never much altered its character. It feels, like Kyoto in Japan, a repository of everything lasting and traditional, and it even has its own legal code, inherited from the Kandyan kingdom of old.

Its fulcrum is the Temple of the Tooth, one of the supremely sacred shrines of Buddhism, in whose inner sanctuary, layered in precious woods and metals, and surrounded by a moat full of turtles, there is preserved a tooth of the Lord Buddha. It is not really a tooth, and its temple, a high confectionery building that reminds me of the Victor Emmanuel memorial in Rome, is not really very beautiful: but the ancient sanctity of the relic gives an extra beauty to the little city, reclining most serenely about this holy place.

Cosy chalets of the British speckle the hillsides all around the lake

Ceylon

like suburbs in Surrey, and echoing out of the valley you can often hear the ceaseless chanting of Buddhist priests in a seminary far below. On the edge of the city lies one of the loveliest gardens in the world, Peredeniya, and through the hills there wander delightful rural promenades, trodden out by dainty Victorian feet, and named for great ladies of the British Raj—Lady Horton's Walk, Lady Gregory's Road, Lady Longden's Drive. Kandy is the sort of place most of us would feel fairly happy to grow old in, and from its example you might suppose that the whole of Ceylon was a kind of half-pay paradise, trellised, embowered and sung in by priests.

It is not so. Outward from Kandy, more or less the centre of the island, the landscapes of Ceylon burst away in over-powering variety —landscapes cruel, seductive, grand or intimate in turn, so intricately jammed together that in a morning's journey you can pass from jungle to alp to classic tropical foreshore. The southern centre of the island is a massed jumble of mountains, with the holy Adam's Peak, where the butterflies go to die, standing there like a fang pre-eminent —visible, as a sacred mountain should be, not only to the buried thatched villages of the forest, but also to sailors out at sea. Tea gardens clothe these highlands, their big white factories facing this way and that across the valleys: and as you drive through the estates, whose big bobbing baskets above the shrubbery show where the tea-pickers are at work—as you travel through the brilliant atmosphere of mountain Ceylon, translucent blue and sudden green, the toasted smell of tea leaves follows you, factory to factory, as though an elderly but inexorable aunt were after you with the tea-caddy.

Out of the tea gardens into the rolling plains, with clumps of firs and eucalyptus and splendid trout streams. On the edge of this country stands Nuwara Eliya, an ineffable anachronism of a hill station. The Prime Minister of Ceylon has a house up there, surrounded by lovely lawns and rose-beds, along the road from the race-course: and nearby the planters' Hill Club, dimly decorated with prints and stuffed fish, has changed so little with the Asian times that to this day no Ceylonese has been admitted to membership. Nurelya is another world from Kandy. It is like a slightly faded resort in the Scottish Highlands, even to the foliage—even indeed to the Scots, and I was not in the least surprised to notice one day outside the half-timbered Grand Hotel, a car whose Ceylonese number plate flaunted the staunch appendage: 'Argyllshire'.

Away to the west stands Colombo, steamy and straggling around

Ceylon

its harbour. In the south is Galle, once the great entrepot of Ceylon, where a big Dutch fort stands sentinel above the sea, and there are evocations still, in narrow street and rampart, of dhows, burghers and adventurers. On the east coast is Trincomalee, one of the grandest of all harbours, a superb double-yoked bay that could, as the guide-books like to say, shelter entire navies. In the north the scrub country peters out into lowland waste and coastal marsh: and all around the island the glorious beaches lie, fringed conventionally with coconut palms, backed by forests, with rickety fishing hamlets on the banks of creeks, and catamarans drawn up beyond the surf.

Bumpy pot-holed roads link these astonishingly disparate parts with one another. Slow rattly trains labour over impossible gradients. Doomed buses trundle from coast to coast. The package tour has scarcely reached Ceylon yet, the philosophies of tourism are not yet dominant, and the island still feels properly organic. ('Bank Closed' said a chalked blackboard notice when I went to cash a cheque one morning, 'On a/c Full Moon Day'.)

Sometimes the transitions of Ceylon are so abrupt that the colours clash, as though an interior decorator has botched the job: and the emotions of the island, too, are often fierce. The murder rate is among the highest on earth, though crime is nearly always un-premeditated, and is often fired by love or family feud. Even Kandy, that perpetual rest cure of a city, is rich in bloody stories, and when I consulted a horoscope in a magazine there one day, I was not surprised to be warned that 'bodily harm is not outside the orbit of your planetary possibilities today'. The clash of dry mountain air and equatorial humidity seems to make for inner resentments. The original Sinhalese resent the immigrant Tamils, the Buddhists resent the Hindus, each wing of every political party conspiratorially resents the other, and there are two Afro-Asian Solidarity Leagues.

The primitive streak is strong, for all the cultured elite of Ceylon (perhaps the most thoroughly westernized of any Asian ruling class): drum beats on the night air, devil worship, queer straggled bands of forest aborigines still eking out, in a few hidden recesses of the island, their last years of the Dark Ages. A recent Prime Minister of Ceylon was taken to task by the Opposition for consulting an imported Indian magician. 'What's your problem?' asked a recent advertisement in the Colombo Press. 'Be it Love, Marriage, Employment, Domestic Unhappiness, Subdue your enemy, Protection from others,

Ceylon

Achieve Promotions, Success at Examinations, Litigation, Delayed Periods, Desertion—Meet or Write to Government Registered CHARMIST (On Sundays, Arudha Hair Oil Office, Gampola)'.

In partnership, the hair oil and the charms. Ceylon is so dense a country, so dovetailed, so ripe, that it will be generations before the technical civilization of the west finally swamps the place, and I know of nowhere comparably safe or comfortable where you may still feel so close to the gnarled roots of nature. If you have never seen monkeys outside a zoo, their presence along the highways of Ceylon is one of the most delightful experiences of modern travel: so exuberantly, divinely free do they look, as they leap the main road in a couple of bounds, or whisk their babies with merry elegance up a tree-trunk. If an elephant chiefly means to you only a sixpenny ride for the children, or a comic character in an animated cartoon, wait till you see one nobly manipulating logs in a Ceylonese teak forest, or best of all striding in wild grandeur, lordly and untamed, from one forest beat to another.

One can see such animals in greater numbers elsewhere, and in fiercer settings: the glory of Ceylon is that there they exist still in immediate neighbourhood to man himself, in an environment easily accessible and actually rather cramped. The fireflies that waver so haphazard through the shrubbery, as you drink your sundowner, are like friendly envoys from that other world beyond the suburbs, the world of the apes and the elephants: and I once drove five miles through a continuing wavering stream of yellow moths, whose antic progress across Ceylon was a reminder that a right of way is not the exclusive privilege of humans.

And proving this point majestically are the most celebrated of Ceylon's sights and surprises, the great ruined cities of her past—Anuradhapura, Polonnaruwa, Sigiriya—which are wonders on a par with the Pyramids or Machu Picchu, and are frequented now, in their abandonment, by the wild creatures of the bush.

Anuradhapura and Polonnaruwa are huge Buddhist cities of remote antiquity, the one succeeding the other as capital of Ceylon in A.D. 1017. They are astonishing complexes of temple, palace and ceremonial highway, with vast domed sanctuaries rising above the scrub, and dynasties of kings marching through their histories. Sigiriya, though, is something different in kind, and in its hushed purlieus, alone and bee-infested in a desolate landscape of the north-east,

Ceylon

the drama of Ceylon is enacted most excitingly of all. Sigiriya, the Lion Rock, is a gaunt and immense column of granite, 400 feet high. It shows from many miles away, theatrically jutting out of a dun countryside, and at first sight seems only to be one of your geological freaks, like Ayers Rock in Australia, or the mushroom buttes of Arizona.

But it is a historical freak as well. Fifteen centuries ago the young prince Kasyapa, coveting the throne of Ceylon, buried his father the king alive in a wall in his capital at Anuradhapura: but terrified of the revenge of his brother, who was in India, he fled the city and set up his own usurping court on the rock at Sigiriya—literally on the rock, for living as he did in perpetual fear of his life, he built a fortress-palace on the very summit, approached by precipitous staircases up the granite, with an audience chamber up there, luxurious apartments, military quarters, water storage tanks and even elephant stables. Around the base of the rock, within walls and a moat, an attendant city arose: but the parricide king, his courtiers and his courtesans, lived insulated high above in maniac asylum.

The rock may still be climbed, and in a gallery half-way are the celebrated Sigiriya frescoes, erotic portraits of half-nude women, full-bosomed and heavily jewelled, whom some authorities have assumed to be Buddhist vestals, and others women of royal pleasure. Up you go, clutching the iron railings erected in a less hell-for-leather age, and between the enormous sculpted lion's feet which have given the place its name, up staircase after staircase, through gallery upon gallery, until at last you emerge upon the flat surface of the rock. It is about an acre square, terraced still with the remains of the madman's palace, and at your feet the scrub-land of Ceylon lies empty and unchanged.

The hostile world feels impotent indeed, seen from such an eastern Berchtesgaden, and Kasyapa survived up there for eighteen years: but in the end his brother came, and he killed himself while the going was good.

Serendipity: not always happy, but never failing to surprise. You remember the waiter who brought my breakfast near the beginning of this essay? When he had left the room I hastened to fetch my notebook, to record his observations word for word: but while I was away from the breakfast table, that damned crow flapped in through the window, and stole a slice of toast.

DARJEELING

Darjeeling, the most celebrated of the Indian hill stations, is all smallness. It is small physically, of course—hard even to find upon the map of India, so tucked away is it like a trinket on the northern frontiers. But it is still smaller figuratively. It is the most deliberately diminutive town I know, as though it is always trying to make itself less substantial still. One crosses vast scorched plains to reach it from Calcutta, over colossally winding rivers, through a landscape that has no end: but at the foot of the hills Darjeeling sends a toy train to meet you—a gay little blue-painted trundle of a train, which takes you indefatigably puffing and chugging up through the forests and the tea-gardens to the town.

Little people greet you at the top. Little ponies canter about little streets. Hundreds and thousands of merry little children tumble all about you. The town is perched upon a narrow ridge, about 7,000 feet up, with deep gorges falling away on either side, and when I arrived there for the first time I found it swirled all around by cloud. It felt curiously private and self-contained—like a childish fancy, I thought, a folly, a town magically reduced in scale and shut off from the world by vapour: but then as to a crash of drums in a *coup de théâtre*, a gap momentarily appeared in the ever-shifting clouds, and there standing tremendously in the background, their snows flushed pink with sunlight, attended by range upon range of foothills and serenely surveying the expanse of the world, stood the divine mass of the Himalayan mountains.

I saw Darjeeling's point, and cut myself down to size.

Some visitors never see the snow-peaks at all, for they are often invisible for days at a time. Anyway there is no need to go on about them. It is enough to say that to see Kanchenjunga and its peers from Darjeeling, in the cool of the morning, is one of the noblest experiences of travel. It is a kind of vision. It has moved generations of pilgrims to mysticism, and even more to over-writing.

Darjeeling

Yet it is not the spectacle of the Himalayas that sets the style of Darjeeling. It is simply their presence. The town lives in the knowledge of them, and so acknowledges another scale of things. Its littleness is not inferiority complex, but self-awareness, and it gives the community a particular intensity and vivacity. Darjeeling is built in layers, neatly along its ridge like an exhibition town, from the posh hotels and the villas at the top to the jumbled bazaar quarter at the bottom: and all the way down this dense tiered mass of buildings life incessantly buzzes, hums and fizzes. Darjeeling's energies seem to burn the brighter for their smallness, and not a corner of the town is still, or empty, or dull.

It is a place of astonishing cheerfulness. Everybody seems to be feeling simply splendid. Perhaps they all are, for the air is magnificently brilliant, the heat is seldom too hot and the cold not often icy. The nineteenth-century Welshman who first put Darjeeling on the map saw it from the start as a sanatorium, and the Rajah of Sikkim kindly handed it over to the British Governor-General of India 'for the purpose of enabling the servants of his government suffering from sickness to avail themselves of its advantages'. Today Darjeeling's high spirits never seem to flag. The children never stop playing, the youths never end their horse-play, the tourists never tire of clattering hilariously about the town on hired ponies. The cicadas sing all day long in the gardens, and ever and again from down the hill come the hoots and puffs of the little trains (which prefer to travel gregariously, and come merrily up from Siliguri two or three at a time).

To the stranger it all seems intenser, more concentrated than real life, and especially after dark, when the braziers are aglow in the alleys of the bazaar, and the hotel lights comfortably shine above. Then half Darjeeling turns out for a stroll at Chaurasta, a triangular piazza half way along the ridge, and on my own first evening in Darjeeling I went and sat on a bench there, and watched the town go by. Beyond the square the ridge fell away abruptly into the night, and there were only the dark foothills out there, and a suggestion of the snowpeaks, and the stars that now and then appeared in unnatural brilliance through the shifting clouds.

To and fro against this celestial back-drop the people of Darjeeling loitered, strolled and gossiped like Spaniards on their evening promenade, or more exotic Venetians at St. Mark's. There were tall flashing girls in saris and nose-clips. There were brown gnome-like men in fur caps. There were slant-eyed children of astonishing beauty, and boys

Darjeeling

with wild eager faces like Gengis Khan. There were monks, and priests, and soldiers, and grand Indian gentlemen in tweeds, and giggly Indian girls in cotton party frocks. There were mountain porters hastening back from work, carrying rucksacks and tent-poles. There were ancient men with plaited pigtails. There were two hippies, and a nun, and four French tourists, and me watching it all, as in hallucination, from a corner bench beside the bandstand.

It was like a microcosm of the world, assembled up there from the plains and mountains, ushered into that little square, reduced to a neater and more manageable size, and given double shots of adrenalin.

'What is your country?' a man peremptorily demanded, as we met face to face and unavoidably on a narrow hill track, and when I told him Wales, to the west of England, he asked further: 'Is it a high pass to get there?'

Unimaginably high are the passes, indescribably remote the valleys, from which in the century since Captain Lloyd founded Darjeeling, the population of the town has found its way to the ridge. This is a frontier settlement. Some of those snow-peaks are in India proper, some in Sikkim and Bhutan, some in the Kingdom of Nepal, some in the People's Republic of Tibet. The town stands on the edge of mysteries, and its people have migrated from many parts of the eastern Himalaya, and from the plains below. The old sanatorium of the memsahibs is far more nowadays: not merely a celebrated resort, but an important bazaar, a centre of local government and a kind of ethnic demonstration.

No little town in the world can show so many kinds, and types, and manners of people. The little Lepchas, the original inhabitants of the region, are seldom more than five feet high, but immensely strong and agile. The Sherpas from eastern Nepal, the high-altitude porters of Everest and Kanchenjunga, move with an inexorable striding impetus, as though they can't stop. The Tibetans often look immensely sophisticated, trendy almost, ready for any Chelsea discotheque with their flared pants and impeccable complexions. The Gurkhas look soldiers through and through, always marching, even off parade, with head high and chest out. One sees few sleepy or dullard faces among these Mongoloid peoples of the north: all seem eminently capable—straight square-set people, who look as though, deposited in a Brooklyn back-alley or one of the remoter villages of the southern Urals, they would instantly find their feet.

Darjeeling

But they are only one element in the Darjeeling *mélange*. There are many other kinds of Nepalese, for instance—Gurungs, Magars, Tamangs, Newars. There are refugees from Tibet proper, and Indian Army soldiers from the Punjab and Rajasthan. Here comes a slim dark girl in blue pyjamas, who might be Annamese, or perhaps Malay. Here are four Rajput officers of the garrison, with their thin black Sandhurst moustaches and their suede boots. The Hindu holy man beside the lane is smeared mysteriously with yellow ochre. The Bengali family being hoisted on to its ponies is all guileless anticipation, proud young father holding the baby (who wears a pink peaked cap with yellow velvet ribbons), mother in gold and red sari assiduously combing the already immaculate hair of a small boy apparently dressed for an exceptionally extravagant wedding. The eyes that peer at you between bushy beard and bundled turban are, of course, the eyes of a Sikh: the shy porcelain smile from the lady at the next table is a smile from the palm trees and sands of Madras.

In the autumn they have races at Darjeeling, and then one may see this demographic jumble at its most cheerful. The racecourse is endearingly claimed to be the smallest in the world: at the end of a race the competitors run breakneck off the course into the approach road, an unnerving experience for newcomers. The meetings are not very formal. Young men play football in the middle of the track. Between races the horses graze casually on grassy spaces round about. A dribble of racegoers stumbles down the mountain track from the town above, carrying umbrellas and race cards, and a stream of jeeps and rattly taxis blasts its way along the motor-road.

Still, the traditional procedures are honoured. The races are run by the Gymkhana Club of Darjeeling, and in the official stand the Stewards and Judges, mostly Army officers, sit in well-cut elegance with immensely superior ladies. Sometimes the senior steward takes a stroll about the enclosure, moving with the lordly benevolence common to racing bigwigs from Longchamps to Kentucky Downs. The race card is printed with every refinement of the racegoer's jargon and the rules are, of course, severe ('Trainers and Jockeys are hereby notified that Riotous Behaviour, Intemperance, or other Improper Conduct, although not occurring on the Race Course, will be taken cognizance of by the Stewards'). It would take an iconoclast indeed, to defy the decrees of the Darjeeling Gymkhana Club.

But all around that grandstand, swarming about the bookies at their little wooden stands, picnicking up the grassy slopes behind,

Darjeeling

haggling with the sellers of nuts or the purveyors of infallible tips, is the infinite variety of Darjeeling, impervious to regulation. Such a conglomeration of bone structures, life-styles, tastes, gestures! Such a cacophony of voices, deep, cracked, sing-song or bell-like! Such a marvellous fugue of history performed there, in the intersections of history, religion, or ambition that have brought this potpourri of the human kind to place its bets on the fourth race!

The bell rings; the flag drops; hurtling around the track in billows of dust come three or four little Tibetan ponies, ridden at desperate speed and with savage concentration by fierce little high-cheeked jockeys—brilliantly liveried in scarlets and yellows, visors low over their eyes—rocketing around that little track, as the crowd rises tip-toe with excitement, until they shoot out of sight, with cheers, laughter and catcalls, behind the grandstand and off the course. It is as though the scouts of Attila have passed through. The stranger may feel a certain sense of shock, but the stewards do not seem disconcerted. 'Jolly good show', they say to each other. 'Hell of a good race, what?'

For the most dogmatic progressive will not deny to little Darjeeling a tug of nostalgia. It is harmless. It is only a fragrance of earlier times, a Victorian bouquet still lingering up here along the ridge. Darjeeling is largely built in that gabled semi-chalet style so dear to Victorian pleasure-seekers, and imposed upon its gallimaufry of peoples is a decorous, poke-bonnet, tea-and-biscuits style. Nobody in their senses would wish it otherwise. It is an essential part of Darjeeling's minuscule mystique, and used to suggest to me a musical-box town, where pretty little melodies would tinkle in the sunshine, while clockwork figures in top-hats and bustles jerkily proceeded along the Mall. The very names of the place carry this old evocation—the Esplanade, Happy Valley, Step Aside: and the main road to the plains is still known in Darjeeling as the Cart Road.

Some of the hotels are deliciously Victorian. The porridge at the Windamere [*sic*] Hotel is, I am told by unimpeachable authorities, unsurpassed in Scotland, while the tea at the Mount Everest is tea, my dear, just like we *used* to have it. Shopping in Darjeeling, too, is agreeably old-school. Patiently attentive are the assistants, instantly to hand is the chair for memsahib, and one almost expects to find, winging it across the Kashmiri shawls and the Tibetan prayer-wheels, one of those wire-pulley change receptacles one used to see in provincial English drapers' long ago.

Darjeeling

Most of Darjeeling's pleasure (I except the illicit joys of the bazaar quarter) would perfectly satisfy our grandparents. There is the classic pleasure, for instance, which I abstemiously denied myself, of getting up at three in the morning to see the sunrise and the top of Everest from Tiger Hill. There are the pleasures of Excursions to Places of Interest, like Ghoom Rock or Kaventer's Dairy Farm. There are the pleasures of identifying wild flowers and trees, or sketching, or looking at animals in the outdoor zoo (where the Llama and the Siberian Tiger, returning one's inspection morosely from their enclosures, look as though they wish the Victorian era had never dawned). There are pony-rides, of course, and there is miniature golf, and when I was there *Ruddigore* was being performed by the pupils of St. Paul's School.

There is the pleasure of walking. In most of Darjeeling no cars are allowed, and this is one of the walkingest towns on earth. One may walk decorously around the town itself, or through the Botanical Gardens. One may walk into the foothills for a picnic. Or one may, stacking up with tinned pineapple and sleeping bags, engage a team of Sherpas and stride off into the distant mountains. Every year more and more people go trekking from Darjeeling, and a very healthy pastime it must be. 'No place like Darjeeling', one stalwart matron reproachfully observed as, staggering beneath the weight of her accoutrements, she passed me doing nothing in particular over a glass of lemonade—'nowhere like Darjeeling for blowing the cobwebs away!'

As I say, our grandparents would have loved it: and sometimes Darjeeling's scrapbook essence can be, to the sentimental visitor, distinctly moving. On Jalapahar Hill, at the eastern end of the ridge, there is a small military cantonment, complete with parade ground, garrison church and shops for the soldiery. I was once walking through this camp, enjoying its display of the military aesthetic—polished brass, regimental signs in white-washed pebbles, the clump of ammunition boots and the bristle of sergeantly moustaches—when an unexpected sound reached me from the parade ground behind. With a slow and melancholy introductory wail, the Gurkha pipe band broke into the sad, sad music of a Highland lament. I stopped dead in my dusty tracks, and the tears came to my eyes: for what generations of my own people, I thought, had stirred to that music in their exiles long ago, and how strange and sweet and lonely it sounded in these hills of the Indian frontier!

'Can I help you?' inquired a passer-by, seeing me standing there.

Darjeeling

'You are not ill?' Not ill, I assured him as I moved on up the hill. Only susceptible!

Every morning before breakfast I used to walk up Observatory Hill. This wooded hump, rising directly above the Chaurasta, is holy to the Buddhists, who have a shrine upon its summit. All along the steep and winding path to the top mendicants invite the contributions of the pious—grave holy men who bow like archbishops, jolly old crones, coveys of chirpy inquisitive children. Two grinning stone lions guard the entrance to the holy compound, the trees are hung all over with white prayer flags, and mysteriously from the recesses of the shrine one may hear the incessant murmur of prayers and tinkling of bells. There are always people up there. Some are praying, some meditating, some reading sacred scripts, and one I met each day used to stand all alone among the bushes looking towards Tibet and writing in a large black notebook.

If the weather is clear there is a glorious view of Kanchenjunga and its peers, and while they were cooking my eggs in the hotel down below I used to sit on the grass alone and marvel at the immunity of Darjeeling. It has, it seemed to me, *escaped*. It knows its own dimension, and is satisfied. Though its name is famous everywhere, still it remains a small town of the Himalayan foothills, very close to the soil and the temple. There is material squalor enough, but seldom I think despair, still less degradation. The loads may be crippling, but still the porters find the energy to smile. The children and the chickens may be in and out of the kitchen, but the mothers never seem to get cross. The girls laugh as they laboriously chop firewood in the thickets, and the bundles of hay piled upon the backs of the labourers are speckled all over with flowers of pink and blue.

It is as though by an unconscious exertion of values Darjeeling has selected what it wants from the world below, and rejected all the rest. And such is the inner variety of the place, so lavish are its colours, so remote is it even now from the pressures of the industrialized society, that within its own limits it can afford to be tolerant. There is nothing censorious about the place. One may look, behave, dress, believe more or less as one pleases. During my stay in Darjeeling I often saw a young American dressed in the habit of a Buddhist monk. He was studying at a nearby seminary, I was told, and wore the brown cloak, the sandals and the hair-bun as to the manner born. Nobody appeared the least surprised by this anomalous figure, and even his

Darjeeling

father, who was paying him a visit from the States, seemed entirely at home with the phenomenon. 'I'm going to drink, Jimmy,' I heard him saying to his son one day, puffing at his cigar and raising his glass, 'I'm going to drink to all these wonderful, wonderful people of Darjeeling!' (And 'Say,' he tactfully added as he put his glass down, rather hastily I thought, 'is this Indian wine? *Delicious!*')

For there is an innocent merit to the place. One feels better and kinder for a visit to Darjeeling. Those stupendous mountains in the clouds have set the scale right, and adjusted the balance. It's no good fussing, they seem to say. It can't last. And this sententious thought, which occurred to me every morning after ten minutes or so upon the hill, used to remind me that my eggs were waiting for me down the lane—and down I would hurry, past that merry line of beggars, tagged by swarms of children and encouraged by avuncular sages, to where the waiter in his red turban and his polished brass badge, looking anxiously from the dining-room door, was waiting to whisk the cover off my porridge.

FIJI

There is a certain sameness to your paradise islands. Toothy girls smile through garlands of blossom, immemorial customs are re-enacted beside hotel pools, indigestible traditional drinks cannot politely be refused, and along miles and miles of beach the palm trees of the travel posters interminably topple.

Some such jaded thoughts, I confess, crossed my mind when I drove for the first time along the south coast road of Vanua Levu, one of the Fijian islands, towards Kumbulau Point at its eastern tip. This was a standard idyll. They call the road the Hibiscus Highway, and the whole apparatus of tropical delight streamed past us along the way. The beaches were limitlessly coral. The hibiscus gorgeously bloomed. Rain-clouds scudded dramatically across the blue, and from the depths of the copra plantation, sloping shadowy towards the sea, genial brown men chopped coconuts and waved. I found myself wondering what I would get for dinner that night, and had forcibly to revive my sensibilities now and then: for I had been to Arcady before.

At the end of the road my companion, after splitting a can of pineapple juice with me, took me out for a stroll and showed me the view. It was undeniably handsome. The azure gulf was ringed with vivid green: a humped green island lay in the distance, rich green fields and trees ran down to the water's edge, and the very air seemed greenly tinged, in reflection perhaps, giving the whole prospect an aquarium air. It was a fine view indeed, but like many another in the South Seas. There did not seem much to say about it, but I did my best. 'What a lovely view', I said, 'quite lovely. And what happens on that other island, the one over there?'

He believed that tourists should be tourists, and brushed the inquiry aside. That was Rabi, he said brusquely, as though polishing off an irrelevance, that was where the Ocean Islanders lived, who had to leave Ocean Island because of the phosphate diggings, who wanted to be independent, who spoke their own language, who didn't allow

Fiji

anybody else there, who had complained to the United Nations, who were suing the British Government—'but tell me, tell me now, have you had an opportunity to taste our traditional welcome drink, *yaqona*, made from green roots and served in skilfully polished coconut shells? And will you have time to see the inexplicable fire-walkers of Beqa, every first Friday of the month at the Korolevu Beach Hotel?'

Wise visitors to Fiji break away from Paradise. It is not compulsory. Fiji is not one of those atoll groups that are altogether monopolized by the tourist trade. It is a large scattered archipelago, strewn in languorous variety on and around the international date line—the *Fiji Times* calls itself 'The first Newspaper published In The World Every Day', and travellers from the United States wake up in Fiji to the disconcerting realization that somewhere south of Honolulu they skipped the whole of Tuesday. Fiji is on about the same latitude as Rio de Janeiro, or Madagascar—1,300 miles south of the Equator, 1,300 miles north of New Zealand. The islands lie well away from the main traffic routes of history, and until the end of the eighteenth century hardly any Europeans had set eyes on them.

There are 300 islands in this archipelago, and at least a hundred of them are inhabited. From the air they seem to be scattered for hundreds of miles in all directions, islands insubstantial, islands vivid with sugar cane and copra, islands utterly without visible resource— bumpy islands, flat islands, half-submerged coral reef islands, islands so tropically seductive, so palm-fringed, surf-washed and white-roofed, that they look like allegories of escape. In the evening especially, when the shapes of all these islands melt into a mauve imprecision, when the sea looks like blue velvet and the sun goes down in a diffusion of pinks and crimsons, Fiji is without question one of the most obviously beautiful places in the world.

Obvious, because it is not a subtle beauty. This is a full-blooded aesthetic, in Gauguin colours and theatrical outline. Suva, the capital of Fiji, looks from the sea like a Pacific port idealized. There are picturesque island schooners at the quayside, and white tourist liners slipping elegantly in and out, and a scurrying, blazing suggestion of market and bazaar along the foreshore, and immediately behind the town the mountains precipitously rise, looking like coloured cut-outs against the sky, and crowned with a preposterous prominence, called Joske's Thumb, which is like a huge knob of bluish plasticine. Small boys dive for coins, or tumble in and out of moored motor-boats,

Fiji

and often on the edge of the reef a solitary fisherman stands poised with his harpoon. This is Everyman's Pacific, and the cruise passengers, streaming down their gangways not at all sure whether they are in Tahiti or Honolulu, nevertheless glow with the fulfilment of travel, as the white smiles, badinage, squashy vegetables and Traditional Ornaments of the Suva market greet them immediately beside the docks.

For Fiji is aware of its allure, and offers all conveniences—markets immediately to hand, day visits to authentic Fijian villages, welcome libations of *yaqona* at the Tourist Office ('You must clap your hands after each drink—*that's* right!'). Most visitors seem to feel they get their money's worth. Many of them, especially Australians, choose Fiji specifically for the duty-free shopping, here as everywhere epitomized by millions of Japanese transistors being sold by immensely superior young Indians. Before the Second World War, Fiji was visited only by rich tourists of the sort they used to call 'globe-trotters'. Now most Pacific airlines land there, hundreds of cruises call, and around the main islands a regular tourist track has been worn, like the trail of the blindfold Egyptian camels round and round their mills.

Most people nowadays land at Nadi, the international airport on the main island of Viti Levu, and spend their holidays in the neighbouring resort town, or in Suva. Some fly on to the second island, Vanua Levu, or even to outliers like Taveuni or Ovalau. Nearly all stay in the air-conditioned, barbecued and landscaped hotels now universal in the South Pacific, where muscular natives beat tom-toms to announce the advent of the cocktail hour, and the bedside canned Cole Porter is statutorily interrupted now and then by Native Island Songs.

Of its kind it is very good. The fish you see from the glass-bottomed boat cruises really are the most varied, the most weird and the most dazzling in the world, from the stunning Butterfly Cod, all wavering draperies like a Parisian dowager, to the unspeakable Stone Fish, whose body looks like pumice-stone, and whose venom can kill a man in a couple of hours. The fire-walkers at the Korolevu Beach really are inexplicable, treading apparently bemused but altogether unscathed across their hot stones, and successfully defying all the investigations of scientists, anthropologists and visiting Rotarian knowalls. The flowers of Fiji are ravishing. The authentic Fijian villages are charming ensembles of thatch, wood and green space, and though they provide Fijian stew and free transport from all hotels every day

93

Fiji

throughout the tourist season, they still miraculously preserve suggestions of genuine hospitality. The yacht cruises to the off-shore islands, though their crews are tiresomely hearty and their passengers embarrassingly loud, still do sail to some lovely unspoilt strands, through coveys of heavenly islands, and down the line of glorious sentimental sunsets.

Many visitors ask for no more than these highly-practised junketings: but in Fiji more than in most island paradises, as I found when I asked the man about Rabi, it is worth looking beyond the brochures. Tourism has not corroded deeply here, and these are islands far more interesting than the publicity men allow.

For example, they are very wet. This is something the agents do not stress, but it is the rain that sets the true character of Fiji, compensates for the tourist gloss, and gives these islands their lush fascination. If, like me, you prefer your South Seas in Conradian mood, there is nothing to beat the clatter of tropical rain on corrugated iron roofs, or the steamy, mouldy, gourd-like, fibrous smell that exudes from the forest when the sun comes out again. Even the hotel swimming pools look more interesting when the rain is pouring down: for then the ornamental palm trees sway and drip, unexpected shining insects emerge from the lawns, and only a few inebriated globe-trotters, sometimes smoking cigars, plop hazily in and out of the water like seals.

In the days before the British Empire took these islands under its improving wing, Fiji was a great place for the rain-soaked boozer with the clenched cigar—the beachcomber, the remittance man, the easy-profit trader, the 'blackbirder' supplying labour for the sugar plantations—the whole ironically completed by settlements of permanently appalled missionaries, and the unaccredited emissaries of rival Powers. At one time or another the Germans, the Americans, the British and the French all had their stakes in Fiji, and the lovely islands were embroiled in every kind of mayhem.

In those days the chief town was Levuka, on the small island of Ovalau, and though this place has long lost its consequence, seldom sees a tourist and is not on a scheduled air route, still it is alive with memories of that lost and unlamented epoch. It stands squeezed on the foreshore facing east, with hills descending so precipitously behind that some of its streets are no more than steep flights of steps disconcertingly dropping out of the bush. Around the harbour stand

Fiji

the memorials of the old Pacific—customs sheds instinct with skull-duggery, warehouses smelling of sacking and opportunism, the fish-packing station, the waterfront pub, the Indian tailor and the Chinese joiner. Here are the stores of the great South Sea traders, Burns Philp, Morris, Hedstrom, whose names are known throughout the Pacific, and from its eminence up Mission Hill Road the Methodist Church still looks warily down, in figurative pince-nez, upon the goings-on below. A century ago this remote port was the focus of the brief South Seas cotton boom; in the 1870s it was the capital of its own Fijian Kingdom; and even now it retains a faintly rakish or knowing air, like a setting for Somerset Maugham.

And this manner of worldly, possibly illicit, sophistication is apparent all over Fiji. The Fijians themselves are an urbane people; the Indian community is wonderfully acquisitive; many of the Europeans are still recognizably related to those frayed but imperturbable adventurers of old. Even in small towns of the out-islands, like Savusavu on Vanua Levu, life feels far from bucolic. The trading community is mostly Indian or Chinese, and displays an unimpressed, even patronizing, attitude to visitors from abroad: it comes as a shock to realize, after half an hour's intense discussion of world affairs with a citizen of Savusavu, say, to discover that he has never in his life stepped outside the confines of Vanua Levu. Most Fijian towns are on the sea, and are visited regularly by island freighters, with British captains and island-hopping travellers of every nationality: many have their own air-strip, with daily flights by the slim little Herons of Fiji Airlines, wavering in like frail toys over the sea. Fiji is not at all a backwater. Its villages may be simple, many of its people are poor, but its temper is startlingly urbane. There seem to be very few fools in the 300 islands: and so far as I could tell, not a single innocent.

One of the exhibits in the little Fiji Museum in the grounds of Government House in Suva, has an especially beguiling caption. '*Wooden vessel*', it says, '*which was said to be used for sending portions of Rev. Baker's flesh to nearby chiefs*'.

Rev. Baker was eaten in 1867, for it was only about a century ago, when these islands were converted to Christianity, that the Fijians abandoned the practice of cannibalism. They remain a most formidable people: formidable physically, for they are enormous, like wrestlers, formidable in personality, for they are endlessly cheerful, inexhaustibly inquisitive, unshakeably loyal and unaffectedly kind.

Fiji

One would not mind being eaten in Fiji. The pot would be spiced, the cooking gentle, and the occasion in most ways merry.

Wide-eyed and open-handed they greet you now, in their tidy thatched settlements off the highway, or among the mangrove swamps where the women, hitching their skirts up to their waists, scoop about indelicately for shellfish. 'Where are you going? What is your name? Are you married? Where do you live? Have you any children? Would you like a banana?' Their curiosity ranges from the self-educational ('How many people live in London?') to the frankly intimate ('Do you sleep alone?') and is directed at you with urgency: the Fijian for curiosity is *via kila*—knowledge-want. The Fijians are easily moved, to amusement or compassion. I told the maids in my Suva hotel that I was scared of them, because they stared at me so hard, and in the evening I found a little bowl of flowers placed beneath my window in appeasement. 'Aaaah', they said, shaking their big kind heads in remorse, 'we no wish to frighten you!'

The Fijians are immensely proud of being Fijian, and they live still by the tenets of a tribal society—owning land communally, honouring their own chiefs, acting always as a community. Their past was fearfully bloodthirsty. They constantly fought each other, tribe against tribe, island against island, and they sailed about the archipelago in terrible war canoes, and brandished huge clubs, and danced alarming war-dances, and ate each other with a more than ritual enjoyment—one Viti Levu chief claimed to have eaten 999 human beings. Unwanted old people were sometimes buried alive, human sacrifice was common, and the indigenous paganism of the Fijians was all mixed up with sorcery and witchcraft.

Yet almost to a man, after the British take-over in 1874, the Fijians professed Christianity, and today their old savagery is sublimated in harmless virility. They are admirable soldiers, passionate Rugby players, enormously hard-hitting cricketers. There is no more reassuring constabulary in the world than the Fiji Police Force, whose officers go bareheaded and wear fringed linen kilts, and who look perfectly capable still of stewing the toughest criminal. During the Second World War, when two Fiji infantry battalions fought in the Solomon Islands, one Fijian soldier was shot through the head, bayoneted twice through the chest and once through the arm, left in a foxhole for three days during an artillery barrage—and lived happily ever after.

There was a time, briefly in the 1870s, when Fiji had a king—

Fiji

Cakobau, who established his capital in Levuka, and claimed paramountcy over all the islands. Cakobau flew his own flag, commanded his own armies and fleets of canoes, issued his own currency and negotiated treaties with foreign powers: stamp catalogues list his postage stamps, with a big CR on them and a crown, in carmine rose and deep yellow-green. His kingdom only lasted three years, giving way by its own desire to the vaster sovereignty of Queen Victoria: but it is remembered still, and the Fijian sense of nationhood has never faded.

Its mystic, rather secretive character is partly sustained by the strangeness of Fijian culture—the fire-walking, the calling of turtles from the deep, the complex nature of chieftaincy. For foreigners it is reinforced too by the Fijian language, whose orthography was devised by missionaries, and is baffling in the extreme. 'B' is pronounced 'mb' in this perverse system, 'q' is pronounced 'ngg', 'c' is pronounced 'th'. Nadi, the airport, comes out as 'Nandi', and Fijian studies are not made easier by the discovery that Cakobau and Thakombau are one and the same king, or that Beqa and Mbengga are the same island all the time.

Most potently of all, I thought, the Fijian pride—so recently descended from bloodshed and magic—was apparent upon the royal island of Bau (or Mbau, if you wish to be pedantic). This was the home of Cakobau himself, is still the residence of the senior Fijian chieftaincy, and represents all that is most classically orthodox and traditional in the Fijian heritage. It is only a few hundred yards from the mainland of Viti Levu. 'Do you know anybody there?' they asked me in Suva before I went. 'You should not really go alone. You must tread carefully'—so that when I found myself being ferried all alone across the Styx-like channel I felt a trifle apprehensive—especially as Charon at the stern of the canoe, paddling slowly across the still water, stared at me throughout in an unnerving silence.

And when I disembarked, Bau *was* rather ominous. I found nothing but kindness there—a sage to welcome me ashore, a boy to show me round, smiles all round from the inhabitants, washing their clothes at waterside steps, or poised in massive elegance outside their doorways. But the numen of Bau seemed to me disturbing: it is a very old, very queer sort of island, where the Fijian style is preserved in a mortuary sensation, and old dead kings seem to be watching you.

The island is very small, perhaps a couple of acres, but rises abruptly to a central hill. The flat space at the bottom is straight-

Fiji

forward enough, its green expanse flanked by a white Methodist church, a handsome thatched council hall, and some magnificent trees. It is up the hill that the eeriness begins. There are not many buildings at the top, only the school and a hut or two, but a powerful sense of unseen presence haunts the place, and leads one through tall grasses and overhanging foliage, along a twisty track above the sea, until on the rainswept summit of the island, overlooking the waterside residence of the present paramount chief below, one comes across the graves of Cakobau and his wife, stone slabs with headstones in the soggy grass.

I thought this a sinister place. The school children waved and laughed as we went down the hill again, but I was glad to be leaving. I had noticed in the church a rough tall stone standing in the middle of the nave, with a small declivity scooped in the top of it. It was the font, said my guide. Funny font, said I. It is a stone, he said. Peculiar stone, said I. He left it at that, and away I was paddled to the mainland, pausing only to embark three heavily skirted women who, laughing hilariously and dropping packages all over the place, waded out to join us: but when I returned to Suva I made inquiries about that stone, and discovered it to be the sacred object upon which, in my grandfather's time, the Fijians used to dash their captured enemies' heads, before, I suppose, stewing them.

'We are Fijian!' they proudly say, and they mean it in a frankly racial sense: in the century since the British assumed their dominion over Fiji, the original inhabitants have been outnumbered by immigrant people. For every 100 Fijians in Fiji there are some 120 Indians— farmers, artisans, professional men, traders so astute that they dominate the retail commerce of the islands: and since there are also Chinese, Europeans, and immigrants from several other Pacific groups, the true natives stand in a distinct minority.

This makes for an odd ambivalence. Though the Fijiness of Fiji remains dominant, as pungent in tourist spectacles as in emanations of Bau, it is interwoven with elaborate cosmopolitan threads— bearded Sikhs at their ploughs, lithe Gujerati tailors, Chinese travel agents, shirt-sleeved Britons sweating in pubs, Australian planters, American bankers, and all that indeterminate polyglot tide of riff-raff and photographers which flows fitfully through all tropical islands. Half the delight of Fiji is provided by this intricate mish-mash of races and manners, and lesser anomalies like those litigious islanders

Fiji

of Rabi fall, when one gets to know the islands better, into a much more ordinary perspective. Fiji is the complex hub of a complex region. Fiji Airlines like to say they serve one Independent State (Western Samoa), one Protectorate (the Solomons), one Condominium (the New Hebrides), one Colony (Gilbert and Ellice), one Kingdom (Tonga), one Republic (Nauru)—and Fiji itself, of course, an independent Dominion of the Commonwealth, recognizing Queen Elizabeth of England as its monarch.

Fiji is segregationist. In these islands all races are equal, but distinctly separate. Fijians, Indians and the rest have their own electoral rolls, and send their own members to a common legislature. They go to their own schools. They speak their own languages. Young people nowadays intermarry, but generally the communities remain distinct—Fijians Christian, Indians mostly Hindu, Europeans beyond religious analysis. While this obviously makes for latent tensions, especially as until recently the Indian birth rate was far higher than the Fijian, it also gives the islands a wonderful patchwork feeling. There is no more invigorating dialectic than that of Fijian political journalism, where the inner factions of Fijian affairs snarl at each other with eighteenth-century abandon: and aesthetically too the racial *mélange* of Fiji, sari beside mini, hawk nose and tremendous biceps, soft Cantonese and incomprehensible Fijian, high spirits of tribal *bonhomie* or melancholy introspection of Bengal—aesthetically this potpourri of styles seems to me just as satisfying as the sunsets themselves, in their rich golden substance down the bay, or that spectacular heap of mountains, like a landscape of royal legend, behind the waterfront of Suva.

'Fiji for Swingers!' say the brochures. 'A Fun Resort with a Romantic Tropical Atmosphere'. I found its wrinkles more fascinating than its smiles, and especially that sense of inner complication tucked away behind the air-conditioning. Even the fauna of Fiji seems more than usually individualist. Its range is surprisingly limited—the flying-fox and a sort of rat are the only indigenous mammals—but its habits are startling. The giant toad is cannibalistic. The annelid seaworm emerges from the sea-reef with astronomical punctuality twice a year, at full moon (and makes allowance, every twenty-eight years, for the difference between lunar and solar time). Both eels and turtles in Fiji respond to the human voice, and will rise to the surface when summoned with the proper traditional call.

Fiji

On my way back from Kumbulau Point that day I discovered that the zip of my jeans had broken, and since I planned to call upon the missionaries at Savusavu I got out another pair and scrambled into the bush to change. Just as I had removed the first pair, and was about to pull the others on, in all that wobbly discomfort, that catching of materials and losing of shoes that goes with the changing of trousers in the middle of woods, I heard a rustling and heavy breathing in the bush. I froze. The noise grew closer. I held my breath. The bushes laboriously parted, and snuffling head down through the foliage there appeared, taking no notice of me at all, a small speckled Fijian pig: on his back stood a mynah bird, intermittently pecking, and together the pair of them, swaying a little, snorting and occasionally squawking, disappeared into the bushes and out of my life.

ICELAND

They get up unexpectedly late in Iceland, and there were few people about when I left my hotel and walked through the streets of Heimaey, in the Westmann Islands. One or two trucks clattered down to the harbour, a few early workers hurried preoccupied towards the fish meal factory, but the little grey houses were mostly silent and lifeless, their lace curtains decorously drawn.

Past the graveyard I walked, where stunted conifers were encased in protective stockades against the wind, and the children's graves blazed with artificial roses: and across the meadows above the town, stopping to greet the sheep entombed in their winter bunker of turf, stone and corrugated iron—the dim interior of the shack thick with their breath, their wide wondering eyes staring back at me through the crack in the door. The snow was quite deep up there on the hillside, and the world lay white and crisp around me, the wide pale vault of the Arctic sky above, away to the north the glacial immensities of the mainland. Birds sang twitchily, a hooter sounded from the factory below, and presently, reaching a ridge that opened to my view to the south, I saw in the distance the sea on fire.

Not smouldering, nor even sparking, but furiously ablaze—smoke streaming from the sea, flashes of red flame, a plume of black bent by the wind until it lay almost parallel with the water. The sea in those parts is littered with squarish lumps of island, dressed in the winter with a crust of snow, and disposed at artistic intervals, as though a Zen seascape master has arranged them there: among them, like a phoenix in that water-garden, the island volcano of Sturtsey raged day and night. Fire and ice and a cold blue ocean. A steam-hammer was thumping now, somewhere in the town, a morning stir was filling the streets, and turning my back upon that prodigy I presently sat down to an Icelandic breakfast—rye bread, cheese and marmalade, served by a ravishingly lovely girl on a preternaturally clean tablecloth to the sound of radio music.

Iceland

The weirdness of Sturtsey is nothing new. Fire and ice and fierce seas have always been the staples of Icelandic legend, and old representations of the island invariably show it dominated by the violent glow of Hekla, the great volcano of the southern mainland. There is something allegorical about the very fact of Iceland, something that puts most visitors in mind of still remoter grandeurs— Dantean visions of heaven or hell, or classical conceptions of Elysium, improbably transplanted to these icy realms with asphodels among the glaciers. This is an island of absolutes, where nothing is blurred, and sometimes it feels less like a country than a prophecy, a mystery play, or a topsy-turvy sort of Utopia.

Iceland is a large island almost in the middle of the North Atlantic, poised equivocally between Europe and America, and so near Greenland that in the summer they run day excursions there. It is rather larger than Portugal, and looks rather like a chunk of the moon sliced off and dropped in the ocean—so like it that early American astronauts were taken there to give them a foretaste of moonfall. The island is not so cold as it looks or sounds. The Arctic Circle passes just to the north of the Icelandic mainland, and the Gulf Stream warms its shores. It is, though, a violent country. A thousand volcanoes have pitted its landscapes with craters, jagged lava lumps, wildernesses of grey basalt. The ferocious winds of the north have kept it almost treeless, only a few scraggy thickets or cosseted garden rowans pathetically surviving the blast. About an eighth of the island is one vast snowfield, the Vatnajökull, which is itself about the size of Corsica, and sweeps away in grand sterile silence from the peak of Hekla.

In summer this colossal landscape is clothed in a fragile green, speckled with wild flowers and charmed by the song of one of Europe's richest bird populations—salmon leaping in its glacial streams, the glorious little ponies of Iceland gliding Pegasian through a crystal sunlight. In the winter the snow falls like a clamp upon the island, closing the rough roads of the interior and filling, like saucepans, the shallow craters of extinct volcanoes. Summer or winter the weather is startlingly changeable. One moment the sky is an incomparable northern blue, and the girls are tanning themselves on the park benches: the next a mad wind is driving sleet and mist wildly through the streets, and one reads in the morning that the farmers have been feeding their animals on all fours themselves, unable to stand upright for the blizzard. Through it all, heat-wave or snow-storm, the geysers and hot springs of Iceland bubble and fume

Iceland

away—some in the middle of Reykjavik itself, the capital, so that citizens bathe in open-air pools all the year round, and heat their homes with subterranean steam, some away in the desolations of the interior, their clouds of vapour billowing from the bare mountain-side, or hissing malignantly out of thick sulphurous pools.

Most of Iceland is uninhabited desert, and the people nearly all live along the coast, around the narrow fjords and river estuaries. In most countries the sea is only an accessory. In Iceland it is a living presence, more vital than the landscape. The Icelanders depend upon it utterly, for their income comes almost entirely from fishing. The Atlantic is inescapable, and the smell of fish hangs everywhere— from the trawlers in every harbour, from the racks of drying cod, head-down in their thousands on the outskirts of every town, from the pickled whale and dried shark on the restaurant menus, from the terrible fish meal factories, malodorous steam issuing from their every crack and manhole, where ghastly things go on with bangs and clanks of machinery.

Even Reykjavik, where more than a third of the Icelanders live, is recognizably a fish-port still. It has its Parliament, its Lutheran cathedral of corrugated iron, its university and its national museum, its villas spreading into the stark countryside around: but look down the main street of the city from the main square, only a stone's throw from the Cabinet offices or the National Library, and there blocking the vista stand the ships, an essential part of the city scene. The trawlers chug in and out of town as familiar as suburban buses, the trucks bounce out of the docks loaded deep with herring, and the stink of the fish factory at the end of the quay hovers perpetually over that end of town—'Mm', say the Icelanders appreciatively, 'the *money-smell . . .*'

They are a people hard-headed but fey, and love to boast of their Celtic blood. The Icelanders are an odd mixture of the urbane and the primitive, or for that matter ugliness and allure. Beauty and the Beast is one of the Icelandic allegories. Everybody who goes to the island is struck by the splendour of the girls. Pick a choice example now—the shopgirl, say, who is packing up your stuffed puffin in the souvenir shop, or pricing your lava-stone powder-box. What a gorgeous strapping girl she is, what a terrific golden girl, with her wide-apart eyes, her hair bleached in Arctic sunshine, her exquisite complexion mixed out of snow and pink blossom! Take your eye off

Iceland

her for a moment, though, and observe the young man now shambling down the street outside—towards his trawler, perhaps, or off to his fearful shift at the fish factory. He is the original Viking, I suppose. He looks like a very determined specimen of Neanderthal man: his forehead and his chin symmetrically recede, his cheeks are wolfishly sunken, his eyes blaze, and there is to his loping walk a suggestion of immense loose-limbed power, as though a tap on his shoulder would unleash his two-headed battle-axe, and send him instantly off to Greenland with horns on his head.

From these disparate strains the Icelander has emerged. He is part Norseman, part Celt, and is very conscious of everything appertaining to race—pedigrees, national characteristics, cross-strains, inherited aptitudes. The very first Icelanders were hermits, who came to these inconceivably inhospitable shores from Ireland, and settled in caves to cogitate. They were succeeded, in the ninth and tenth centuries, by Viking adventurers, Norwegian by stock but often accompanied by wives and slaves from Ireland and the Scottish isles. The Danes became rulers of Iceland in the fourteenth century, and since then almost no alien blood has joined the Icelandic stream (except when the allied soldiery was here in the Second World War). Ethnically the Icelanders are all on their own, and not much like anybody else. Many peoples suppose themselves extraordinary—the English, the Americans, the French, the Swedes, they all like to think that the rest of the world considers them eccentric. Of the peoples I know the only ones who really seem to me a little mad, in the engaging sense of easy-going dottiness, are the Icelanders. They are full of surprise—very quiet at first acquaintance, so that you may wonder if you have displeased them in some way, by talking too loud or wearing the wrong colour, but unpredictably bursting into uninhibited *bonhomie*, with gargantuan toasts and awful hangovers.

Perhaps the long northern winters are the cause, and that cage of the winds above one's head. It is as though the Icelanders feel a physical need, every now and then, to break into carnival or even bacchanal. They are great drinkers, and even greater lovers. Love is approved of in Iceland. In the old days, when the fisherman's life was short and dangerous, there were always more men than women, and free love was a social necessity. Today it is a respected tradition. Illegitimacy is no disgrace, and most young people live together before marriage—'Rooms wanted', runs a familiar small ad in the Icelandic newspapers, 'by engaged couple with baby'.

Iceland

In so small a country, so intricately intermarried, paternity is hard to deny, and most Engaged Couples with Baby seem to live happily ever after: all Iceland knew the facts, some years ago, when the daughter of one eminent politician was made pregnant by the son of another (though in this particular case, I was told, the girl's mother was so distressed that she 'went to bed'—the standard Icelandic solution to problems). Iceland is a very sexy country—a young country, with the highest birth-rate in Europe, and a high-spirited one, where the dances are fast and frequent, and far into the night in Austurvöllur Square, at once the Piccadilly and the Red Square of Reykjavik, the young people linger when the last dance is over—tooting their car horns in the small hours, dancing on the sidewalk outside Parliament, singing what one assumes to be bawdy songs and laughing so boisterously that the foreign visitor to the Borg Hotel, peering from his darkened window on that lusty dalliance below, either pulls his pillow over his head with a pang of lost youth, or hastily gets dressed again.

This streak of excitement, this Celtic ore to the Nordic mass, runs through the life of Iceland. There sit the Parliamentarians at their morning coffee (they drink gallons of coffee in Iceland), and they look senatorial enough. They are big-built, heavy-jawed men in sombre suits, their eyes cold and blue as ice, hunched over their cups and talking, one imagines, about caucuses and constituencies: but if you venture to intrude upon them, announcing yourself a foreigner, you will find a dizzy variety to their conversation. This well-known politician plays the flute, this one is an enthusiastic follower of English football, this one recently translated one of Goldoni's comedies into Icelandic—and presently others will join you, a business man with a taste for oratorio, a journalist turned art dealer, or one of those folk-heroes of modern Iceland, a trawler-skipper, who is likely to look much the most suave of them all, and cherish a particular interest in kinetic abstractionism.

Most sensible foreigners stay at the Borg, if they can spare the money. It is no longer the grandest or dearest hotel in Reykjavik, but it is an institution. It is like a Russian hotel of the old school, very plush, with caryatids to support the wall-lights in the restaurant, and portraits of anonymous Icelandic worthies in the bedrooms. When I stayed there last I often noticed in the foyer an elderly Icelander of appearance at once benign and distracted. He was tall, a little stooped and exceedingly craggy, with a well-worn cravat around his neck,

Iceland

hair flying like snow about his head, and clothes of an Edwardian gypsy elegance. This was Johannes Kjerval, the most famous artist in Iceland, if not in Scandinavia—the greatest painter of the North, Icelanders say. 'He is not like other men', somebody warned me. 'He is very strange in Icelandic, and will be stranger still in English.' I introduced myself nonetheless, and so it proved to be. A strange, marvellous man! He had moved into the hotel from his own house, he told me, because 'I have lost my sleeping there, and can't catch it'. Sometimes his conversation struck mysteriously off into Italian, a muffled sort of French, and English doggerel of his own composition; sometimes he fell into a smiling silence, or produced a vast wad of papers from an inside pocket to show me a reproduction of a painting. Whatever he did there was an immense power to his presence—an unpredictable force, which seemed to me, like his art and his old-fashioned cravat, disconcertingly but movingly Icelandic.

Patriotism burns fiercely in the island. This is distinctly their own, their native land, and they are born last-ditchers and never-say-diers. It is only a generation since they gained their full independence from the Danes—the Germans had occupied Denmark, the British had occupied Iceland, and the Republic was proclaimed after a national referendum. Until the 1850s, Danish control had been so absolute, in this then poverty-stricken island, that there was actually a Crown monopoly of trade, and virtually every shop-keeper in Iceland was a Dane from Denmark. The Icelanders themselves were so little regarded, and their attachment to their homeland seemed to the Danes so unlikely, that at one time there was talk of shipping them all off to Denmark, and leaving the island to the elements once more, or the hermits.

Now there is little hard feeling against the Danes, and a faintly Danish patina is still apparent. A stone crown of Denmark still ornaments the Parliament building, and the sense of humour which distinguishes the Danes from their fellow-Scandinavians still echoes in this spirited little State. The national pride of the Icelanders is far older than mere politics. It revolves around the Icelandic language. Through many centuries it was the ancient literature of Iceland, cherished by word of mouth, which kept the Icelandic nationality alive, and enabled the distinctive Icelandic culture to survive. Above all the sagas, the great prose narratives of medieval Iceland, embody the spirit of this people: those high-flown tales, half fact, half fiction,

Iceland

which commemorate the families and heroes of Viking Iceland, and form a priceless repository of history, mythology and romance. The language of the sagas has survived intact, and is still the everyday speech of the people. If an Icelander can read today's paper, he can read the Njalasaga, a tragedy of Icelandic life at least six centuries old. There are no dialects in Icelandic, and no accents of class: to the foreigner it looks like some kind of Esperanto, the sort of language in which one can often bluff or worry one's way to comprehension—if *kalfahryggjarvodvi, skeinka og egg*, may defeat one, at least *vinstukan er opin daglega* fairly obviously announces that one can get a drink any day of the week.

A mystic exaltation, not without comedy, surrounds this hallowed tongue. Committees of dedicated sages devise new words, when the vocabulary proves inadequate to the times: a military tank is a *skidreki*—'creeping dragon'. Bards abound, people launch themselves without warning into poetic declamation, the tales of Nils the Law Man or Grettir the noble robber are as familiar to Icelandic children today as they were to the Icelanders of the Middle Ages, crouched enthralled over their peat-fires as the story-tellers postured on. The Icelandic language and its literature links every era of island history with the next, and enables almost every islander to trace his origins gloriously back to the poets, kings and navigators of antiquity.

This makes for an extraordinary sense of continuity. Iceland is one of the very few European countries where elderly women still wear national costume as a matter of course—a dress of shiny black and gold embroidery, a bodice laced over a coloured blouse, worn with braided hair and a tasselled velvet cap to give a dauntingly Wagnerian effect. The ages are truncated in Iceland. People speak to you of Grimur Goatbeard or Leif the Lucky as though they are neighbours up the road, or first cousins once removed. I first went to Thingvellir, the site of the ancient Icelandic Parliament, on a lovely summer day in the company of an elderly Icelandic business man. He looked an ordinarily respectable citizen, and seemed indeed rather too prosaic a companion for the occasion, when we drove through the scowling declivity in the rocks that gives access to the place: but once we stood on the edge of Thingvellir, and looked across that wide lava plain, flecked with green and shining with reflected sunlight from its lake, my companion seemed to be lyrically transformed, and in lofty terms and a rather booming voice peopled the scene

Iceland

before me with the heroes and poets of old, Eilif the Eagle and Audun the Bald, the wandering bards, the explorers home from the west, the young athletes in the sunshine. I viewed him with a new respect, but on the way home all he talked about was the national balance of payments.

Every Icelander seems to know every other Icelander, even if a century separates them. It is like a family of intense internal loyalty, welded together by generations of hard times. There are virtually no surnames proper in Iceland, only patronymics—you merely add your own to your father's christian name, and become Stefan Jónsson, for example, or Sigrid Jonsdóttir. This means that an immense number of people have the same name, like Joneses in Wales; and like the Welsh, the Icelanders identify themselves by their trade—'I'm Kjarval the Painter', they will say, and the telephone directory too adds a calling to the subscriber's name, to differentiate Olaf Stefansson the Dentist from Olaf Stefansson the Ships' Chandler. Class differences scarcely exist, in an island where everybody seems to claim descent from Ornold Fish-Driver or Sigurd Snake-Eye, and there is little sense of gulf between young and old. All are, so to speak, members. The only Icelandic titles are bestowed upon bishops and priests—a clergyman is Sir Priest, like Shakespeare's clerics—and children are admitted to responsibility at astonishingly early ages. Nothing is more surprising in Iceland than to hand over one's fare in a country bus and find it accepted by a character apparently not much more than four years old, who deposits it solemnly in an enormous satchel, peels off a ticket and grumbles with absolute adult authenticity if you haven't got the right change. Privacy is not much in demand, in so egalitarian a society. Even private funerals are broadcast on the State radio, for a fee, enabling the entire nation to share the family grief.

Iceland has no army, no air force and only a vestigial navy, but there are few countries of more militant outlook. The Icelanders have never fought a war in their history, at least since Viking times, but they seem ready to take on all comers any day, in defence of the cod and the sagas. Their island has a fortress air, and there is a touch of regimental discipline to their society. It is forbidden to adopt surnames other than patronymics. It is forbidden to keep dogs, except on farms. The absolute equality of life gives the place a paradoxical uniformity—there are no stately homes and no hovels, no millionaires and nobody on the dole. This little nation has a manner of faintly

Iceland

fanatic conviction, like a proselyte to some new and urgent faith. One evening in Akureyri, on the northern coast, I heard the sound of solemn singing emerging from a restaurant, and peering through the door I saw that a large party was in progress. Akureyri has a reputation for particular reserve, and I felt as I looked in as though I were physically separate from those rituals, on the other side of the goldfish glass. There the Icelanders sat in ordered ranks, their arms linked around the long tables, and as they sang what seemed to be some kind of sacramental anthem, or Viking marching song perhaps, they swayed heavily from side to side in a rhythmic motion. It gave me a queer impression of secret solidarity. Everybody knew the words of the song, and the whole assembly seemed to be in arcane collusion: I noticed that if ever I caught an eye, as the celebrants sang and swayed there at the table, after a moment's puzzled focusing it abruptly switched away from me, as if to dismiss an illusion.

I like a robust national spirit, though, especially in little nations that can do no harm with it. I enjoy the Icelanders' jealous insularity, and am not in the least offended when they seem to think I must be some mistake. Sometimes indeed the closeted intimacy of Iceland possesses great beauty. The President of the Republic lives in a farmhouse built by the Danes on a spit of land outside the capital, and a visit to this official residence, especially in winter, hauntingly illustrates the aloof self-sufficiency of Iceland. No head of state could live more simply. The house is a pleasant gentleman-farmer's sort of establishment, with a conservatory against one wall, a pair of antlers above the garage door, and a clutter of impeccable farm buildings behind. There is a little white steepled church in which the President will one day be buried, and the swallow-tailed flag of Government, red and white on dark blue, flies from a flagpole on a terrace. Neat little paths have been cleared in the snow around the property, to keep the Presidential spats dry.

All around this modest homestead the white flat shore, melting into the sea, is speckled with farms not quite so big as the First Citizen's house, but not much different in kind—neighbourly looking houses, whose families, one feels, might easily pop over to His Excellency's for a schnapps or a game of bridge in the evenings. To the south, superb glacial mountains heave along the horizon; pinks and icy blues and dazzling morning whites. To the north, beneath the rampart of Mount Esja, Reykjavik stands upon its bay like an Arctic Alexandria. Before long, very likely, the fickle Icelandic weather will

Iceland

change, and the view will be obliterated by fierce driving mist or stinging hail: but a glimpse is enough of that silent prospect from the Presidential farm, to show what Iceland's independence means.

Iceland stands on the fringe of European civilization, but not beyond it. In some ways it is less insular than Britain, and is rather like a Baltic State without the Russian or German influence. It is an outrider of Europe. I went to church one Sunday in the Lutheran Cathedral at Rejkjavik, and sat in the gallery beside the choir. The music was exceptionally beautiful. The pastor in his white ruff sang the prayers with a tragic richness of tone, like a fair-skinned rabbi, and the organist suggested to me a figure from some Baroque music-school, or the Kapellmeister of a princely court in old Germany. He was young, grave, long-faced, with a high forehead and wavy ginger-ish hair falling over his collar at the back. I could not take my eyes off him, as he strode with splendid assurance into the Bach fugue that ended the service, so paradoxically did he remind me of greater cities and other traditions far away: and sure enough, when I mentioned him to a friend later I learnt that he stood in direct professional descent, by way of successive masters and pupils, to an organist of Bach's own church in Leipzig.

The Icelanders are not cultural chauvinists. Haldar Laxness, the most celebrated modern Icelandic writer, told a story of an Icelandic singer whose supposed fame in the world at large, which made him a national hero at home, was in fact altogether spurious—a satire on provincial values set in the Iceland of fifty years ago. In those days Reykjavik was a tiny town that knew no better. Today, Iceland, like one of those fervent literary and debating societies one comes across in lumber camps or polar settlements, is earnestly in touch with every intellectual movement, and pressing always on the heels of the avant-garde. The Icelanders buy, and publish, more books per head than anyone else in Europe, and no best-seller, in any western language, long escapes translation into Icelandic.

They are very musical, too—part of their Celtic heritage, no doubt. There is a national symphony orchestra, with musicians imported from Britain or the Continent to augment the local talent, and choral societies, string orchestras or at least gramophone clubs spring into existence in the most improbable fishing hamlets. Professional musicians are much respected. At the airport one day I noticed among my fellow-passengers a well known Icelandic opera singer whom I

Iceland

had heard in a concert the day before, and was now off to sing in Germany. He had looked imposing enough on the platform, but in the flesh and the camel-hair coat, with his admirers clustered around him, the airline officials solicitous and the general public awe-struck, he seemed a very Napoleon: when I thanked him for the beauty of his performance he bowed with superb condescension, as though to compliment me upon my finesse in first removing my gloves.

On the other hand most Icelanders appear to have no sense of visual fitness, and Iceland is perhaps the most unpicturesque country in Europe. Its people have never had the gift of blending their buildings organically to the environment. Even the old gabled farmhouses seem to sit awkwardly upon the surface of the land, in no way integrated to its folds and colours, and the small towns and villages are almost uniformly plain. No tottering merchants' mansions, timbered and aromatic, stand upon the quayside at Reykjavik, as they do across the water in Bergen: no quaint pubs or thatched seafarers' cottages give character to the fishing towns of the east. Concrete is the Icelander's building material now, and his favourite style might be described as Bourgeois Functional—square, that is, with picture windows. The hot springs and geysers of Iceland are so abundant that at one village, Hveragerdi, they grow grapes, bananas and passion flowers under glass: yet very few Reykjavik householders bother to have greenhouses of their own, to soften the angular greyness of their city—'we would do it for business', they say, 'but we have no time for hobbies'.

For the Icelanders like money. A century ago life here was as hard as it could be anywhere, and the comforts of Copenhagen or London must have seemed utterly unattainable. Now the Icelandic standard of living is among the highest in Europe. The fabulous earnings of the herring fishermen, with their new electronic aids, have forced up the standards of everybody else. To the visitor, Iceland seems cripplingly expensive, but hardly any Icelanders are poor. They are a generous people, and self-indulgent too: a classic sight of Icelandic life is that of a party of fishermen at the Naust restaurant, the most famous on the island—pale, plump young men they generally are, after their weeks at sea, but buoyantly high-spirited, swilling away the schnapps with gusto, eating gargantuan meals of steaks or lobster-tails, and looking as though they have simultaneously survived a war of decimation and come into a fortune.

Iceland

Iceland is *nouveau riche* in an agreeable sense. It has suddenly
come into its own. It has leapt from miserable poverty into wealth,
from provincial ignorance into cosmopolitan awareness. This gives
it an air of tingling opportunity, and has its effect on almost everything. Fifty years ago there were no painters in Iceland, and precious
few paintings: now scarcely a living-room in the Republic is without
its water-colour Hekla, its fluffy kittens in baskets or its multi-
coloured visions of piety. Fifty years ago most Icelanders lived, like
the Westmann Island sheep, in cabins of basalt and turf: now they
have nearly all moved into houses so excessively decorous, so frilled
about with lace and potted plants, so ineradically tidy, that one
wonders where the children ever go, to spill their paints or distribute
their space-helmets. There has never been a public railway in Iceland, but from horses and sledges the Icelanders have leapt so
exuberantly into cars and aeroplanes that hardly anybody walks anywhere, and the visiting Briton is chaffed for his dogged pedestrianism,
when he decides to take a turn around the square.

It has all gone delightfully to the Icelanders' heads. They blow
their car horns more guilelessly than anyone, they listen to music more
intently, they load their walls with more pictures, they read more
books, have more babies, eat more food. They seem to laugh more
than most people—and sleep more. Their lovely little ponies, a
generation ago the only means of country locomotion, are now
creatures of pleasure, trotting about on Sunday mornings with gum-
booted young Icelanders on their backs. Their snow-slopes, once un-
visited from one year to the next, are now littered with little trolls on
skis. One can almost feel the new ideas arriving, the latest skirt
lengths and the most experimental dramas, as the aircraft from
London and New York sweep in low over Reykjavik to land. 'If we
must be vulgarized', say the more liberal of the old hands, 'let us at
least be *internationally* vulgar!'

Fortunately the touch of innocence remains. This is too small a
community for cynicism, and the extraordinary nature of the terrain
means that Iceland can never be quite like other nations, however
congested the traffic crossing of Reykjavik, or thronged with group
tours the distant glaciers. A proper corrective to the glittering new
affluence is a visit to the Althing, which claims the oldest pedigree of
any Parliament, and sits in its nice little grey assembly house next
door to the Cathedral. No pomp and little circumstance attends the
deliberations of the Althing. If it is winter the members' goloshes are

Iceland

parked neatly outside the chamber door, and in the public gallery loungers cheerfully read the morning newspapers or climb over the wooden benches to chat with friends nearer the front. Icelandic politics can be vicious enough, but the parliamentarians rarely burst into invective, perhaps because they are nearly all each others' cousins, and often in armchairs at the side of the chamber men may be comfortably smoking their pipes, for all the world as though they have dropped by for a family discussion. Occasionally a page hastens in, with a quotation for the Foreign Minister, perhaps, or a statistic for the Minister of Finance; but he is likely to be wearing a check shirt, a green jersey and corduroy trousers, and as often as not he interrupts the flow of debate by banging the door behind him. Nobody minds. Drat the boy, one seems to hear them murmuring. His father was just the same.

IRELAND

On a football Saturday night O'Connell Street in Dublin must be the most rollicking main street in Europe: glaring with snack-bar lights and fan-club favours, loud with drunks and opportunist evangelists, with its buskers playing their flutes upon its bridge, its wild-eyed bravos in from the bog, its begger-urchins falling upon the astonished tourists with whines and repartee as they emerge from the lobby of the Gresham hotel. It is a scene of terrific fustian activity, and its energies, its enthusiasm, its noises and its faces are undiluted Irish.

Not long ago this was the grandest thoroughfare in the most elegant of the English imperial cities. Then Sackville Street, given grace by the foresight of the Dublin Wide Streets Commission, was given dignity by the presence of the Anglo-Irish, a ruling caste from across the sea. Nelson stood serene on his column outside the G.P.O. Young gentlemen in hacking jackets sauntered over the bridge from Trinity College. A different *class* of customer, as the up-stage head porters used to say—'if you get my meaning sorr'—was to be seen upon the terrace of the Gresham. A symmetry had been laid upon Ireland, and an alien Empire imposed its style, its standards and its conceptions of order upon the little capital.

In the story of the British Empire, Ireland plays a part of tragic prominence, as the oldest of the British possessions overseas, and the first to break away: and it was in the pursuit of an imperial quest that I set out from the Gresham myself one recent day, patting the urchins kindly on their grubby heads, to divert their attention. I wanted to discover what had happened to the Anglo-Irish. Did that imperial caste survive? Were its values buoyant still, behind the republican façade? Was there still a Sackville Street, beneath the changed names and the demolished statues? Or had the Anglo-Irish been absorbed at last into the melée of the football crowd, their manners smudged and their chiselled features blurred? (For they were in their heyday, so Engels reported in the 1850s, tall, strong, handsome chaps, 'with enormous moustaches under colossal Roman noses'.)

Ireland

I presented myself first at St. Patrick's in Dublin, Dean Swift's Cathedral, which was the ancient shrine of this elite. Of all the Empire's Anglican Cathedrals, each in a sense deprived of its meaning, this seems to me the most telling. They were no transient expatriates, who worshipped here in the old days. The rulers of the Protestant Ascendancy represented an imperial presence seven centuries old. They were the most loathed of all the Empire-builders, and at the same time the most rooted, and all the ironies of their relationship with Ireland linger among the trophies and memorials of this cathedral, where the Knights of St. Patrick once sat emblazoned in the stalls of their Order, and Guinnesses bowed only to Viceroys.

The survivors were not numerous at Matins, but they looked staunch enough. 'Kneel to Pray', enjoined the hassocks severely in embroidered capitals, and only the American tourists found the exertion beyond them, the local old ladies plumping down with scarcely a creak. The hymns went lustily (though I was sorry we did not sing No. 313 in the Church of Ireland hymnal—*Lift Thy Banner, Church of Erin, To Thine Ancient Faith We Cling*—which would have expressed a fighting spirit, I thought, in a country of 104,000 Anglicans to 3,200,000 Catholics). The sermon was about universal degeneracy. A fierce lady beside me, observing me faltering with my prayer-book, thrust her own into my hand with a decisive injunction about the number of the psalm. Across the aisle a very military worshipper, attended by his floral-printed wife, stood for the Creed at a classical regimental attention, thumbs down the seams of his brown check trousers, in a posture that would have satisfied any martinet colonel of the Connaughts in the glory days of long ago. There were some elderly men who looked like stewards of jockey clubs, or retired Collectors of Patna; there were two families of such utter Englishness that in any other outposts of Empire I would have assumed them to have been representatives of Shell; there was a sprinkling of those weedy liturgically-buttoned young men always to be found in naves of the Anglican persuasion. It was a congregation of very pronounced character—conservative, perhaps a little arrogant, but faded.

Only a generation ago these were the rulers of Ireland. More still, to an extraordinary degree they were the progenitors of the British Empire as a whole. If the rank-and-file of Victoria's army was largely Irish Catholic, its leadership was habitually Anglo-Irish Protestant. Wellington, the Napiers, Roberts, Wolseley, Kitchener—all these

Ireland

British generals came from Ireland, and without them the Victorian Empire would never have been conquered. At the same time it was paradoxically Anglo-Irishmen, though of many social backgrounds, who gave form to the spirit of nationalism within the Empire, and thus decreed its fall: among the Anglo-Irish nationalists of Ireland were Wolfe Tone, Parnell, Casement, Pearse, even Douglas Hyde, the Gaelic-speaking first president of Eire. There were times—parts of the eighteenth century, for example, and those years of 'terrible beauty' in the first quarter of this century—when the gifts of the Ascendancy made Ireland one of the most exciting countries in Europe: for the clash of loyalties in Ireland brought out the spirit in the Anglo-Irish, and made them in their merits as in their faults more vivid than most.

'Ascendancy' was a weak word for their standing in their prime. Descended partly from Normans, partly from English and Scots 'planted' in Ireland by successive schemes of colonization, they formed a governing class of absolute supremacy. Most of the land was in their hands, the indigenous Irish aristocracy having generally disappeared, and the few industries that flourished were mostly Protestant-owned. Though often impoverished themselves, the Anglo-Irish inherited the habits and instincts of privilege. By the mid-Victorian era, when their separate origins had been fused into a common culture, they were a people like no other—neither quite English nor properly Irish, full of fizz, courageous, humorous, sometimes brutal. A ghastly sequence of historical events had either hardened them into insensitivity, or given them an unexpected tenderness: for they had witnessed, from the vantage-point of their isolation in the land, all the miseries of the Great Famine and the Land Wars, the conflicts of patriotism and coercion, the alternate stiffening and weakening of British resolve in Ireland. They knew imperialism from both sides, and had grown up with its dilemmas.

I thought of them all, so frequently larger than life, as the sermon passed from student violence to get-rich-quick. I thought of the shameless absentee landlords, and the cruel black-and-tans, and those tiresome vocational Anglo-Irishmen who can still, even now, be so unavoidable in pubs. I thought of the Galway Blazers, so called because their members, during a celebratory hunt carousal, burnt down Dooley's Hotel at Birr. I remembered Lord Charles Beresford's imagery for the effect of buckshot fire upon an Arab's bald head at the battle of Abu Klea—'riddled', the young officer imaginatively thought, 'like the rose of a water-pot'. I considered the unyielding detestation that this people had inspired among the exiled Irish of the world— still to be experienced in Sydney or in Boston, or heavy on the air of Grosse Isle outside Montreal, where the refugees from the Great Famine crawled ashore from their ships half-dead with hunger and disease, encouraged by jigging fiddlers.

But I remembered too little Lord Roberts, 'our Bobs', whom the soldiers loved; and the tremendous Lawrence brothers, who ruled the Punjab with God-like conviction; and C. J. Napier of Sind, who so cherished his subject peoples of the Ionian Islands that he named his daughter Cephalonia; and dear old General Butler, husband of Lady Butler the military painter, who was haunted all his life by memories of Irish evictions, and who unfortunately for his success as Com-mander-in-Chief in South Africa, agreed with the Boers; and Mr. Richard Holmes of the Gibraltar Gas Company, a prominent Irish member of the Calpe Hunt who not only preferred to tailor his own pinks, but also engraved his own hunt buttons, made his own boots and saddlery, and was killed happily hunting in 1888, aged 76.

For the Anglo-Irish usually went to extremes, if not of ferocity or sympathy, then simply of fun. Perhaps it was in response to some inner conflict: for though they formed an occupying caste in their homeland, foreign to its working people and commonly hated by them, still they often loved the island with a tortured intensity. That twisted love and pride haunts St. Patrick's, and when the service was over I stayed behind in its cool dimness to contemplate the monu-ments. The congregation stumped out, to exchange brisk pleasantries in the porch. Inside its predecessors rested—the proconsuls and the administrators, the Ever Esteemed Judges and the Eternally Beloved Mothers, Swift himself finally at peace in the nave, generations of Royal Irish with their sculpted wolfhounds sleeping at their feet. There they lay dispossessed—Respected no longer By All Members of The Community, and hardly Universally Mourned.

The voluntary ended and a silence ensued, broken only by those shuffling, clicking and gasping noises peculiar to organ-lofts when their work is done. I took a last look at the frieze of the Sive Dagon Pagoda in Boormah (captured 1852), paid my last respects to Lord Mayo, Viceroy of India (assassinated 1872), saluted the filmy standard of the Connaught Rangers (disbanded 1922), and went out into the bitter Dublin sunshine.

Ireland

They had been for the most part country people—land-owners of varying grandeur, agents to great estates, country clergy, soldiers: so into the country I went next day, and was struck first by the melancholy of their absence. Their long demesne walls still march forbiddingly beside the country roads, but they are all too often crumbled, crudely patched, or replaced in reconstituted stone by expatriate Germans. Their churches smell of must and neglect. Their country houses—seldom very luxurious, being notorious for draughts and rats—are frequently derelict. Around their relics the island's busy new life regardlessly proceeds, no longer needing the gentry up at the great house, or even much resenting their memory.

I went to Birr, where the third Lord Rosse coped bravely with nineteenth-century unemployment by having a moat dug around his demesne, and where he built in the middle of his park the biggest telescope in the world—the Giant Telescope of Birr. The moat is still there, the sixth Lord Rosse occupies the castle, the lovely gardens are open to the public: but in a green declivity there monumentally reclines, blackened with age, the huge iron tube of the Giant Telescope, supported on brick piers—an object almost unnaturally of another Irish age, when a rich Anglo-Irish amateur, from a trough in his King's Country demesne, could still be the first to resolve the stars of the Owl Nebula.

I went to Kilkenny, where the great castle-seat of the Ormondes stands at the opposite end of the place from Irishtown. The Club House Hotel preserves its memories of hunt ball and gentlemanly high jinks, with cartoons of eminent members of the Establishment, and brown photographs of celebrated meets: but the Ascendancy has long vanished from its dining-rooms, where only the Catholic families tumultuously eat their high teas, and a lavish priest at the corner table says grace over his own dinner. At Kilkenny School, a nice Georgian house down by the river, were educated such great men of Anglo-Ireland as Congreve, Farquahar, Bishop Berkeley and even Admiral Beatty of Jutland: but its pupils nowadays are from Protestant farming families of modest means and pretensions, indistinguishable from Irish Catholics except, I fancied, in a certain restraint or muffling of demeanour.

I went to Mallow, once the raciest of Anglo-Irish spas, where the young bloods of the eighteenth century gambled and horse-played their inheritances away with enviable abandon: but only the little spa house bears wistful testimony to the Rakes, in mock-modest half-

Ireland

timber like a French queen's dairy, with a line of washing behind. I walked sadly through the ruined gardens of Coole, up the great avenue of yews and ilexes, where Shaw and Yeats and Keats had loitered in the great days of the Irish renaissance, to scratch their initials on the celebrated copper beech: but all is overgrown and unkempt now, with young trees sprouting everywhere among the rosebeds, and the house itself was demolished in 1941. I went to Tyrone House on the Galway coast, for several centuries the seat of the St. George family, now only an immense four-square ruin against the Connemara hills—the surviving St. Georges only ordinary farmers now, over Kilcogan way, their forebears having gone native. ('But it could be a fine house still', I remarked to a passer-by—'what a place for a ball!' 'O wouldn't you say it was too late', the Irishman picturesquely replied, 'for that kind of fandango?')

And I made a pilgrimage to Ross House, the old home of the Martin family, whose tall façade one can see over the trees from the road between Galway and Oughterard. I had read, in Mr. Maurice Collis's *Somerville and Ross*, an unforgettable letter from Violet Martin describing the return of her family to this house in 1888, after a long exile in Dublin. Mrs. Martin was met in the hall by an elderly tenant, Mr. Paddy Griffith, and together they danced a jig at the foot of the stairs, the dignified Anglo-Irish lady and the merry Catholic dependent, encouraged by the watching housemaid with cries of 'Dance, Paddy!' Mrs. Martin was wearing, I don't know why, a pink dressing gown and a black lilac-trimmed hat, and carried a spade under her arm: and together the two of them skipped and charged about the hall, bowing and curtseying to each other.

Ross is overpoweringly Anglo-Irish. I found it deserted, when I got there on a wet and windy afternoon—a foreigner had bought it, I was told, but seldom came near the house—'God knows what will become of it, more's the shame'. The drive was rutted and overgrown, and the wind blew in gusts across the little lake, flattening the reeds and raising small grey-green waves. It is not a large house, but it has force. A row of servants' quarters flank it, like slave quarters in other imperial parts, and around it a bare and roughish park extends. The house, standing like an oblong box on end, possesses an amateurish grandeur—carriage sweep, ornamental urns, stone benches beside the portal: as I walked up the wide steps to the front door, huddled against the wind, with the trees creaking and the windows rattling, it seemed to me almost stagily evocative.

Ireland

I peered through the dirty windows into the hall. All was dingy inside, half-furnished, the bare staircase rising to the left of the hall, a door at the side to the kitchen quarters. It looked as though nobody had been interested in the house for a couple of generations: but as I squinted through the glass, cupping my hands about my eyes against the reflection of the park behind, I distinctly made out a flash of pink and lilac, a kick of leather leggings, a suggestion of white linen half-way up the stairs: and I thought I heard a sweet Irish voice on the wind—'*Dance, Paddy, Dance!*'

Yet more substantial ghosts survive. Numbers of Anglo-Irish patricians still call Ireland home, and here and there one may find the lost culture of the Ascendancy still vigorously alive. I visited one house in County Cork which remains a perfect paragon of the style. It is a low square house, with a salmon stream running through its park, built around an open courtyard through whose archway tractors chug and trailers rumble. The estate is a picture of prosperous activity, almost Burgundian in that soft warm air of the south, its fruit and vegetable orchards and gardens bent over by diligent employees, its hedges and lawns immaculate, every vista preserved, every door-knob polished. Its agent lunched with us and talked about the neighbours, suggesting to me, as Ireland so often does, a page in a Russian novel. But its true glory is its library: not one of your standard country-house libraries, stocked with unopened classics and forgotten theologians, but a superbly equipped and replenished collection of books—books beautifully shelved and categorized, books just opened from the booksellers' wrappings, books properly used, cherished and understood—a private library of the highest European class, reflecting a degree of civilized resource that no purely indigenous Irish household has yet been able to achieve.

Of course few of the Anglo-Irish were ever so cultured, and a far more common survival today is the home of the aged imperialist, home from the forgotten frontiers to his father's house. Ireland in imperial times was a haven for the half-pay officer, the unentailed younger son, who could not afford or attain to the spacious life in England. Many an Irish house is still full of the Benares brasswork, ivory elephants, monkey-skin shields that mark the imperialist retirement, growing a little tarnished or mildewed now as the last imperial generation grows old: the second-hand bookshops of Ireland are wonderfully fertile in imperial memoirs and guides to sporting

opportunities in the tropics. There is a suggestion of parody to the
relicts of this doubly expatriate society, and I sometimes heard echoes
of East Africa or British Columbia, as I listened for the tribal calls to
Ireland. 'Ready for dins?' I heard one lady ask her repulsive spaniel,
as we waited together for the lift in Galway: and 'You'd never know
he was a shooting dog', she predictably added, when the little beast
rose upon its hind legs to slobber upon the porter.

I had been told years before of a village called Castletownshend in
County Cork, in which the mystique of the Anglo-Irish was said to
survive encapsulated. It was, they told me, a text-book example of the
genre, where I could sense better than anywhere else the quality of
enclave which characterized the lives of the caste. The Anglo-Irish
lived, wherever they were, separately. Many were excellent landlords,
many were genuinely attached to the Irish peasantry, but only a few
families, like the St. Georges of Tyrone House, lived on terms of
genuine equality with their Catholic neighbours. In Norman times the
Pale, the expanse of verdant country around Dublin, was reserved
for them. Later they ensconced themselves in those country estates
beside whose lodges a mailbox is often obsequiously positioned,
like the private railway halts of magnates in England.

To Castletownshend I made my way, and found it to be one of the
prettiest villages in Ireland. A single main street leads down to its
haven, with a residential castle and a Protestant church at one end,
and what used to be called 'gentlemen's houses' scattered throughout. It was the home of Edith Somerville, Violet Martin's colleague
in the partnership Somerville and Ross, and it has long been dominated by two closely connected Anglo-Irish families, the Townshends
and the Somervilles.

The Anglo-Irish did not often congregate in villages, but Castletownshend is a remarkable exception. It is a solid bloc of Anglo-Irish
traditions, values, styles and memories. On one wall of the church a
vast three-column tablet, several thousand words long, traces the
descent of the Townshends, and is punctuated with evocative phrases
of the Ascendancy, like 'Eton and Christ Church', 'of colonial
extraction', or 'the third Lord Lyveden's younger brother'. On other
walls the Somervilles predominate, and we are reminded of Castletownshend men fighting in wars from the Napoleonic to the Hitlerian,
governing territories of hideous remoteness, sitting in Admiralty
Courts or being Bishops. Edith Somerville used to play the organ in

Ireland

this church, and in a house down the road Admiral Boyle Somerville, R.N., was murdered by gunmen in 1936.

Townshends and Somervilles, I very soon discovered, still dominate the village. Pews are still reserved, a notice in the church porch told me, for Mr. Salter-Townshend and Brigadier Somerville (not to speak of Brigadier Becher, Captain Chavasse, Air Vice-Marshal Botts, Colonel Whitmarsh and Miss Penrose-Fitzgerald). Mrs. Salter-Townshend remains chatelaine of the castle, at one end of the village, Brigadier Somerville is master of Drishane, at the other. Between the two sundry ancillary Somervilles flourish, several lesser Townshend homesteads thrive, and by present reckoning, I was told, the two old houses have inter-married fifteen times. In the Second World War, neutral though the Republic stood, their men went off as always to His Majesty's forces, taking with them an astonishingly large proportion of the Catholic Irish population: and the families remain, it appears, uninhibited by history. It is true that the castle now accepts holiday guests in summer, and that the younger Townshends and Somervilles mostly go away to work, returning to the village only for holidays: but they apparently call it home still, and most of it remains family property. The Salter-Townshends live in their waterside castle surrounded by the trophies, paintings, books and family trees of their imperial heritage: and when they meet in the street they greet each other traditionally—'Morning, Cousin Robert!'—and swop the family news with as much gusto as ever they did in the old days, when Boyle Somerville's destroyers were often to be seen lying in the bay at the end of the garden, and Edith pulled out all the stops for Hymn 313.

But the Anglo-Irish as a clan always were recognizably Irish as well as ineradicably Anglo. Whether they were descended from Elizabethan magnates like the Ormondes of Kilkenny, or superannuated Victorian majors, a mutation subtly affected their style, making them at once harder and less inhibited than ordinary Englishmen. In some Anglo-Irishmen nowadays the process has clearly gone a stage further. The Irish is predominant: the Anglo takes second place. In the end this will probably be the destiny of the whole caste—to subside into their environment like those exiled aristocrats to be found in some islands of the British Caribbean, who have long since lost their lofty bearing, and are poor whites like any others. When I returned to Dublin I put the thought to an Anglo-Irish friend of mine, who certainly showed no signs of subsiding himself, but was nevertheless, I would guess, a good deal more Irish than his father had been. How soon, I wondered, would the whole Anglo-Irish caste go native?

Not just yet, he seemed to think. 'What do you suppose the President of Ireland would do', he asked, 'if one of your Anglo-Irish peers, his hands red with the blood of history, were presented to him in Arus an Uachtarain? D'you think he'd throw him out? He'd be grateful to his Lordship for condescending to call'. There is still, it seems, even in this brave new republic, social cachet to a touch of the old style. The new Irish bourgeoisie looks to me more like a West German middle class than anything else, puffing at its cigars between the courses of excessively fattening meals: but a respect for hierarchy apparently survives (and it was after all an Irishman who described *Ulysses* as 'the inevitable result of extending university education to the wrong sort of people').

Economically the Ascendancy is still powerful. In Ireland as in South Africa, it is only in recent years that the British monopoly of big business has been cracked, and there are still banks, companies and industries generally recognized as Anglo-Irish. Dublin still has its traditionally Anglo-Irish newspaper, college, even hospital: it is curious how many institutions in the capital still carry the prefix Royal, from the Hibernian Academy to the Zoological Society. One cannot look up all these things in a directory; the nuances are delicate; but the Anglo-Irish presence remains part of the grain of Irish life, and worldly Dubliners well know which committee is likely to be Protestant dominated, which business has Anglo-Irish directors, and which litterateur, however rich his dialect or flaming his patriotism, is descended from Archdeacons.

But it is a transient and ambiguous role. The Anglo-Irish are powerless politically in Ireland, and seem reconciled to the fact. They wisely stayed neutral in the Troubles, and they generally acknowledge the fair treatment they have since had from the Republic. This must make their loyalties hard to resolve. 'Do you *think* of yourself as Irish?' I asked one youngish Anglo-Irish land-owner, and he looked a little annoyed at the question. 'Don't you think I have a right to', he retorted, 'when my family has been here for 400 years?' I wasn't at all sure, for I knew that he travelled on a British passport, had a son at Eton, and spent a large part of his time in London: but I feel sure that his children will feel obliged to opt one way or the other, Irish or

Ireland

English, monarchist or republican, Commonwealth or what the Foreign Office used to call Non-Foreign Country.

For Ireland has found an identity again. In the early 1960s Dublin struck me as a sadly stagnant city, still harking back to the excitements of rebellion, and painfully self-conscious about its independence. Now the republic has proved itself. Dublin, though it no longer shakes the world with art or politics, has recovered its native vivacity, and the Saturday night football crowd, surging so boisterously past the site of Nelson's column, properly represents the national momentum. Before it the Anglo-Irish, Engels' handsome hawk-nosed fellows, can only retreat—growing less identifiable each year, as their purpose disappears and their historical meaning grows dim. Like many another imperial settler colony, the Ascendancy is declining into legend.

On my last day in Dublin I was taken to its principal surviving bastion in the capital, the Kildare Street Club, Woodward's glorious Venetian palace overlooking Trinity College, from whose great sash windows generations of Anglo-Irish looked fastidiously down upon the civic goings-on. I found it much as I had hoped. It was rather dark and fairly empty, and hung with sporting pictures, and with the crests of all the Knights of St. Patrick, whose less heraldic perquisites included honorary membership of the club. The people I met seemed well in character too: an explosively entertaining novelist, a comfortable peer of the Irish creation, a character straight from Ben Travers who had recently inherited £25,000 and instantly spent it ('People often come up and say look old boy, how much was it really, they tell me it was quarter of a million. *Far* more than that, I say').

'I guess this must be the National Museum', an American paterfamilias is alleged to have said, wandering with his family into this club one morning: and it is a kind of museum—an Ark of that disinherited society, full of its shades and artifacts, its tales and its prejudices. Its pleasures are less social than anthropological, like the rituals of Ashanti. Some years ago its members sold half their premises to an insurance company, and they did not scruple to include the very room through whose window, according to hallowed legend, W. G. Grace once drove a cricket ball from the Trinity College pitch. When I heard this I knew my job was done, so I packed my bags and took to the ferry: for nowhere else in the old imperial territories could they treat so powerful a fetish with such heedless abandon.

KASHMIR

It was in Kashmir, late in travel and half-way through life, that I first went transcendental. Reality seems distinctly relative in that high and timeless vale, truth bends, distance is imprecise, and even the calendar seems to swing indeterminately by, week blurred into week and Friday arriving unannounced upon the heels of Sunday night.

For my first few days I stuck to the facts, but ever less tenaciously. Nobody else seemed to find it necessary. No decision seemed sacrosanct there, and life was apparently suspended in some limbo between events. I lived myself on a lake of no particular shape or exact location, linked by meandering reedy waterways to a fifteenth-century city down the valley. It took me an hour to get to town, reclining full-length in the cushioned recesses of a boat, while the paddle-man behind me sang high-pitched melodies to himself, took occasional gurgles at a water-pipe, and drank green tea with salt in it. Sometimes I stopped to make an improbable purchase—a jade bangle, a duck for dinner, a chunk of honey off the comb. Sometimes perfect strangers asked me how old my watch was, or told me about their forthcoming examinations in elementary economics. Sometimes, having spent the whole day maundering about the city, I returned to my lake late in the evening with not the slightest recollection of anything specific having happened to me at all.

So in the end I emancipated myself, and soared unimpeded beyond actuality, seldom quite sure where I was, or when, or even sometimes who—answering all questions with abandoned fancy, never seeking a reason or providing a cause. I felt myself disembodied between the green-blue lake and the snow mountains all around, in a gentle Nirvana of my own: nowhere existed, it seemed to me, beyond the celestial vale of Kashmir, and whether the vale existed itself was a matter of individual perception.

I was not the first to enter this airy plane of sensibility. Kashmir has been having such an effect upon its visitors for at least 400 years.

Kashmir

The Moghul emperors, who conquered it in the sixteenth century, responded to the vale with a sensual passion, embellishing it with seductive gardens and honouring it with royal dalliances. The British, who became its suzerains in the 1840s, thought it the ultimate retreat from the burdens of empire, and took its magic home with them to the strains of *Pale Hands I Loved, Beside the Shalimar*. To-day's wandering hippies find themselves rootlessly at ease there, and Middle Americans who spend a couple of Kashmir days between Treetops and Hong Kong often feel the interlude to have been an insubstantial dream.

Kashmir has always been more than a mere place. It has the quality of an experience, or a state of mind, or perhaps an ideal. The Muslim sectarians called the Ahmadiya believe that Christ did not die upon the Cross, but was spirited away to Kashmir, the last haven of perfection: and the Moghul emperor Jehangir expressed the wish on his deathbed that Kashmir and Paradise would turn out to be, as he had always thought, one and the same place.

In my more lucid moments, I must here interject, I did not *altogether* agree with the Emperor. Looked at hard and realistically, Kashmir falls short of Elysium. Situated as it is high in central Asia, north of Tibet, squeezed between Russia, China and Afghanistan, it can hardly escape the world's contagion. Beside the golf course at Srinagar, Kashmir's capital, one often sees the waiting white cars of the United Nations, chauffeurs patient at the wheel: and there are soldiers about always, and angry politicians, and students with grievances, and unpersuadable men of religion. Kashmir is one of the world's perennial trouble-spots. Though its people are mostly Muslims, it was ruled until 1947, under the aegis of the British, by a Hindu dynasty of Maharajahs: since then it has been disputed by India and Pakistan. The whole of the vale of Kashmir falls within Indian territory, but sizeable chunks of the outer state are governed by Pakistan, and legal sovereignty of the whole has never been decided. Kashmir is one of those places, deposited here and there in awkward corners of the earth, that never seem quite settled: a bazaar rumour kind of place, a U.N. resolution place, a place that nags the lesser headlines down the years, like a family argument never finally resolved.

Besides, in my Paradise nobody will be poor: most of the inhabitants of Kashmir are very poor indeed. My Paradise will always be merry: Kashmir is infused with a haunting melancholy. In my

Kashmir

Paradise there will be no tourist touts, sharks or hawkers: Kashmir, for more than a century one of the great tourist destinations of the earth, boasts the most charmless touts and indefatigable hagglers in Asia. In my Paradise château-bottled burgundy will flow like water: in Kashmir all but the most extravagant of Moghuls must make do with Indian Golconda, sixteen rupees a half-bottle from the vineyards of Hyderabad.

Where was I? Drifting, that's right, all but motionless across a Kashmiri lake, preferably in a shikara. A shikara is a distant relative of the gondola, canopied, low in the water, looking rather stern-heavy and propelled by that boatman with the water-pipe, squatting at the stern. From *outside* a shikara looks like a fairground novelty, brightly coloured and curtained, and generally full of gregarious Indian youths waving and crying 'Hi!', wrongly supposing you to be a research student in comparative ethnology from the University of South Utah. *Inside* the shikara feels a very different vehicle— like a floating capsule or divan, exquisitely cushioned, moving unguently through the water-lilies towards pleasure-gardens and picnics.

Though the vale of Kashmir is 800 miles from the sea, and surrounded on all sides by immense mountains, still its prime and symbolic element is water. The Kashmir thing is essentially a rippling, liquid kind of happening. Geologists say the whole valley was once a lake, and a string of lesser lakes ornaments it still. Srinagar stands in the middle of four, and is criss-crossed too by ancient canals, and intersected by the great river Jhelum. Boats are inescapable in the capital: boats grand or squalid, spanking or derelict; boats thatched, shingled, poled, engined; boats deep with fruit, nuts, timbers, furs, livestock; barges, and punts, and canoes, and skiffs, and elderly motor-boat taxis; above all those floating figures of the Kashmir scene, those vessels of fragrant legend, houseboats.

Kashmiris have always used houseboats of a kind—straw-thatched craft like arks, chock-a-block with cooking-pots, washing-lines and chicken-coops, leaking wood-smoke from their every crack and often ominously clamped together with iron struts. It was the British, though, in the heyday of Empire, who devised the standard Kashmiri house-boat of the love lyrics and the tourist brochures—what one might call the Pale Hands Houseboat. Sensibly denied the right to acquire land in the valley, they took to the water instead, and evolved their

Kashmir

own kind of pleasure-craft. I suspect they based it upon the barges which used to form the club-house of Oxford rowing-clubs—themselves developed from the ceremonial guild barges that once conveyed London aldermen up and down the Thames from board meeting to turtle soup.

The Kashmir version has come to be a sort of chalet-boat, or water-villa. It is often gabled, and shingle-roofed. There is a sun-deck on top, with an awning, and the poop is comfortably cushioned, and has steps down to the water. The boat is generally fitted in a Victorian mode: heavy dark furniture, baths with claw feet, antimacassars very likely, hot water bottles for sure. Each houseboat has its own kitchen-boat moored astern, and its attendant shikara alongside, and its staff of resident servants, and its own special smell of cedar-wood, curry, roses and ingrained cigar-smoke: and living upon such a vessel, moored beside the orchard-bank of Nagin Lake, or lying all among the willows of a Srinagar canal, very soon one finds reality fading. The lap of the water takes over, the quacking of the ducks in the dawn, the hazed blue smoke loitering from the cookboat, the soft water-light, the glitter of the dewdrop in the water-lily leaf, the flick of the little fish in the clear blue water, the dim purplish presence of the mountain beyond the lake, fringed with a line of distant snow.

Time expands in such a setting, and loses its compulsion. The hours dawdle by, as the bearer brings you your coffee on the sun-deck, and the shikara man lies on his own cushions awaiting your instructions, and the peripatetic trading boats sidle into your line of vision—'You like to see my jewelry, madam? Any chocolates, cigarettes, shampoo? You want a very nice suede coat, sir, half the price of Savile Row? Flowers, memsahib? Haircut? Fur hat? Laundry?' Nothing very particular occurs. A meal comes when you want it. The shikara is always there. The ducks quack. If one considers the matter carefully one finds that the sun rises and sets, and some time between tea and sundowner it does begin to get dark.

Scale, on the other hand, contracts. The focus narrows, within the frame of the Kashmir water-life. The picture gets clearer, more exact, and one finds oneself concentrating upon minutiae, like the number of leaves upon the plucked waterweed, or the twitchy movements of the kingfishers. I took Jane Austen's novels with me to the vale of Kashmir, and perfectly with this delicate awareness of the place did her quill dramas and porcelain comedies correspond.

Kashmir

Sometimes, as I say, I was swishily paddled into town. Then through lily-thick channels we proceeded, willows above us, green fields and apple orchards all around, and as we approached the city the texture of life thickened about us. Barge-loads of cattle glided by to market. Infants sploshed about in half-submerged canoes. Women in trailing kerchiefs, neatly folded about the head, cooked in shanty-boats or washed their clothes at water-steps. Solitary fishermen cast their nets in the shallows: sometimes a man paddled an empty punt along, sitting cross-legged and gnomish in the prow. We passed beneath medieval bridges trembling with traffic, and beside tall houses latticed and mysterious, and past open-fronted waterside stores where merchants sat grandly upon divans, smoking hubble-bubbles and bowing condescendingly in one's direction. We paddled our way, like an admiral's yacht at a review, through flotillas of houseboats— *Young Good Luck*, *Winston*, *Kashmir Fun*—all apparently De Luxe With Sanitation, some with tourists jolly on the poop, some all dank and deserted, like funeral boats between rituals.

And presently we found ourselves upon the muddy water of the Jhelum itself, with its parade of old bridges (Zero Bridge to Eighth Bridge) and the brown jumble of Srinagar all around: distractedly I would disembark to loiter through the labyrinth of the bazaars— pursued by suggestions proper and profane, and seldom knowing where I was going. Though Srinagar is only seventy minutes from Delhi by daily jet, yet it is a frontier town of Central Asia. Here since the start of history the caravans from Sinkiang or Kazakhstan rested on their way to India, and these tangled suks are more like Turkestan than Bengal. Here one feels close to the Uzbegs, the Kurds, the Mongols, the merchants of Tashkent or Bokhara: and often one sees exotic figures from the remotest north swinging through the bazaars, in goat-skin cloaks and fur hats, to remind one of the grand mysteries, Pamir and Hindu Kush, which stand at the head of the valley.

Srinagar has its westernized quarters, of course. It has a golf course, and a grand hotel that was once the Maharaja's palace, and a slightly less grand hotel that the British used to frequent, and a bank with a genuine Scottish manager in an Edwardian villa above the river, and a pleasant waterside esplanade called the Bund, and a Club, and heaps of tourist shops, and a Government Emporium of Kashmiri Crafts—carpets, woodwork, papier mâché, jewelry. There are a couple of cinemas in town, and there is a brand-new Anglican church,

Kashmir

the old one having been burnt down in 1967 in a fairly obscure protest, it seems to me, against the Six Day War.

But downstream from this enclave, strewn around and within the bends of the Jhelum, medieval Srinagar magnificently survives. No addict of the mouldering picturesque could complain about these bazaars. They possess all the classic prerequisites of oriental allure— spiced smells, impenetrable alleys, veiled women, goldsmiths, mosques, sages, dwarfs. The air of old Srinagar is heavy with suggestion, not too closely to be analysed; and its lanes are so crowded with shrouded and turbanned personages, so opaque with dust and smoke and vegetable particles, that invariably I lost my bearings in them, and wandering fruitlessly among the temples and the cloth merchants, over the Third Bridge and back past the tomb of Zain-el-Abdin, at last I used to clamber into a tonga, and went clip-clop back, to the flick of the whip and the smell of horse-sweat, to my patiently waiting shikara at the Dal Gate. 'Houseboat now?' the shikara man would murmur; and back to the lake I would be unnoticeably propelled, eating walnuts all the way.

Yet it has not been an exhilarating progress. The eye of Kashmir is a brooding, almost a baleful, eye—the eye of the shopkeeper, calculating above his wares, the eye of the military policeman on his traffic-stand, the eye of the floating trader, peering ever and again through the houseboat window in search of victims within. The movement of Kashmir is grave and measured, and even the humour of the valley has an enigmatic heaviness, revealingly expressed in shops that call themselves The Worst, or Holy Moses.

The Kashmiris are a hospitable people, but not inspiriting. They seem to be considering always the possibilities of misfortune. In the autumn especially, a lovely season in the valley, the fall of the leaf seems a personal affliction to them, and the passing of the year depresses them like a fading of their own powers. Then in the chill evenings the women disappear to private quarters behind, and the men light their little baskets of charcoal, tuck them under their fustian cloaks and squat morosely in the twilight, their unshaven faces displaying a faint but telling disquiet. 'Come in, come in', they murmur, 'come and join us, you are welcome, sit down, sit down!'— but for myself I generally evaded their sad hospitality, preferring Miss Austen's gaiety on the poop.

Yet I was half-ashamed as I did so, for their kindness is very real,

Kashmir

and all the truer for its reticence—a flick of the head to disclaim
gratitude, a discreetly forgotten bill, an unexpected appearance at the
airport just when you most need someone to hold the typewriter
while you fumble for the porter's tip. There was a touching pathos,
I thought, to the Kashmiri style. 'How do you like your life?' I asked
one new acquaintance there, when we had progressed into intimacy.
'Excellent', he replied with a look of inexpressible regret, 'I love
every minute of it'—and he withdrew a cold hand from the recesses of
his cloak, and waved it listlessly in the air to illustrate his enjoyment.

The vale of Kashmir is like a fourth dimension—outside the ordinary
shape of things. About 100 miles long by twenty miles wide, it is
entirely enclosed by mountains of great height and splendour—a
green scoop in the Himalayan massif, hidden away among the snow-
ranges, desperately inaccessible until the coming of aircraft, and still
magically remote in sensation. The Moghuls, on their holiday pro-
gressions to Srinagar, used to climb with convoys of camels and
elephants over the southern ridges from Delhi. The British generally
came on horseback or in coolie litters over the hill-tracks from the
west. Even today, as you fly effortlessly in from the south, the impact
of the valley is strangely exciting, as you cross the ramparts of the
mountains and see its lakes, its orchards, its great plane trees richly
unfolded there below. It is not exactly an escape—one does not
escape into an enclave. It is a mood of transference or even apotheosis:
a trip without drugs, a pot-less ecstasy.

Kashmir does bear some paradoxical resemblances to other places
far away. The country villages with their thatched tall farmsteads,
their coveys of plump ducks, geese and chickens, their grain-stores
and their woodpiles, look like villages of eastern Europe. The side-
valleys of the mountains, down whose lanes cloaked herdsmen drive
their sheep, goats and ponies in scrambled majesty to the lowlands,
remind me very much of Persia. The waterways of Srinagar suggest
to every visitor some less gilded Venice; the evening cry of the
muezzin, echoing across the lake at dusk, is an echo of Arabia; for
four or five generations every Oxford heart has responded to the
willow-meadows of Kashmir, so like the banks of Isis that one can
almost hear the cricket-balls and transistor radios of *alma mater*.

But these details of the familiar only intensify the oddity of the
whole. There is really nowhere like Kashmir. There are no gardens
so voluptuous as the great Moghul gardens around Dal Lake—

Kashmir

Shalimar and Nishat, Cashma Shahi and Nazim Bagh—intoxicating blends of the formal and the unassuming, grand with terraces and cool with fountains and sweet with roses, with splendid pavilions at the water's edge, and glorious towering trees. There are no ruins so unexpected as the ancient temples of Kashmir, dotted around the valley in astonishing neo-classical elegance—Greek in their grace, Egyptian in their grandeur, uniquely Kashmiri in their flavour. I know of no crop so startling as the saffron crop of Kashmir—acres of purple crocus-like flowers lavishly splashed like mad paintwork across the valley. I know no holy place more disconcerting than the Hindu shrine of Mattan, where hundreds of thousands of sacred carp thresh their lives away in horribly congested pools, jammed tight together in a seething fishy mass. And I shall never forget the wayside stall, north of Srinagar, where I stopped one day to buy something for my supper: it was piled high with the weirdest variety of game-birds I ever saw—ducks of all colours, huge wild geese, black straggly moorhens, and most authentically Kashmiri of all, I thought, a solitary grey heron all folded inside itself, its neck tucked beneath its belly, its legs crumpled below its rump. (No rooks? I asked. No rooks: the Koran forbade it.)

For the ultimate aloofness of Kashmir the traveller must climb to the rim of the valley, to the high alpine meadows of Gulmarg or Pahalgam. There the separateness of the place achieves a disembodied quality, and the whole valley seems to be resting in some high cradle among the clouds, supported by the snow-peaks all around. You have to walk to attain this mystic detachment—away from the little chalet-hotels and bazaars of the resorts, up through the silent pine woods, along the banks of slate-grey trout streams, up through the last crude huts of the highland shepherds, beyond the tree line, over the granite scree until you stand among the snows themselves, on the rampart ridge.

Often the vale below is half-veiled by cloud, and one sees only a green patch here and there, or a suggestion of water: but all around the white mountains stand, holding Kashmir on their hips—peak after peak, ridge after ridge, with Nangar Parbat supreme on the northern flank to set the scale of them all. Kashmir is, as I say, a place like no other: yet even from such a vantage point, high up there in the snow and the sun, its character is curiously negative. It could not possibly be anywhere else: but it might, so it often seemed to me in the hush of those high places, be nowhere at all.

Kashmir

One can judge it only by itself. The fascination of Kashmir is essentially introspective, a mirror-pleasure in which the visitor may see his own self picturesquely reflected, adrift in his shikara among the blossoms and the kingfishers, It is no place for comparisons. Paradise, here as everywhere, is in the mind.

MALTA

hotographs exist of St. Mark's Square in Venice after the campanile had fallen down in 1902, looking forlornly but at first glance inexplicably deprived. I am reminded of them now by the Grand Harbour at Valletta, which really is the grandest of harbours, and is engraved on nearly all our imaginations. Something is missing there too—not a building, but a Fleet. The British battleships lie there no longer, grey and towering at their caissons, broad in the beam but delicate of upperwork, one behind the other beneath the fortress walls. The gay dghajsas no longer flit about cushioned deep with sailors, and the admiral's pinnace does not often chug its haughty way towards a pink gin with His Excellency. For a whole generation of Europeans Malta without the Royal Navy is St. Mark's without the bell-tower: not for any ideological reason, or even necessarily with regret, but simply because those ships seemed as essential to the scene as the ramparts of the Knights themselves. They were part of the architecture.

Now they are gone. Malta, for so many years the headquarters of the British Mediterranean Fleet, has little to show of the British naval presence beyond a flag or two, some mostly Maltese sailors and a portly leading rating I once saw chugging gloriously up French Creek in an inflatable dinghy. Even the brass on the boats of the Grand Harbour Ferry Service, lying in the lee of Fort St. Angelo, is a little tarnished these days: the United Services Sports Club at Marsa, not so long ago one of the jolliest places imaginable, still indeed has parking space reserved for the Captain of Golf, but has sadly lost paint and panache.

There are still British air bases and battalions in Malta, but it was the Navy that really counted, historically and aesthetically. It is true that Nelson originally failed to grasp the strategic meaning of Malta, and at first the British showed no insatiable appetite to possess it, but in the end its connection with the British Empire was essentially a naval affair. The British themselves saw it in terms of firepower,

Malta

fuel and convoy routes: the Maltese thought of the Empire primarily as an employment exchange. Both attitudes were justified by history. For the Empire Malta proved its worth at the very end, when its possession altered the course of the Second World War. For the Maltese the end of Empire was signalized all too clearly by the closure of the Naval dockyard and the threat of destitution.

In Malta the Raj *was* those battleships. The morganatic comradeship of Empire, with India, or Canada, or the tribes of Zululand, must have meant very little to ordinary citizens of this island. The dénouement of Empire is symbolized for the Maltese not by any lowering of ensigns or departure of pro-consuls, but simply by those empty moorings in the Grand Harbour, where *Nelson* and *Warspite*, *Barham* and *Iron Duke* once so majestically lay.

None of the cant phrases of British imperialism applied to Malta. Here there were no hinterlands to be united, no spheres of influence to be established. No civilizing mission was required and the heathen had been redeemed, in a Papist manner of speaking, for centuries. Malta was a fortress, no more, no less. Of course the British adopted an imperial stance there, just as they did in Quebec and the Cape, two other imperial provinces with European cultures of their own. It was psychologically necessary, it seems, for the imperial race to create its own self-sufficient elite. In Quebec the British habitually affected to understand no French. In Malta they erected a kind of imaginary colour-bar (the Maltese being not much swarthier than Welshmen), excluding Maltese from all the best clubs, and seldom inviting them to dinner-parties. Perhaps they found the pretensions of the Maltese aristocracy, which goes in for high-sounding titles of inconceivable antiquity, a trifle comic: they were certainly able to view from an eminence of Protestant condescension the struggles between spiritual and temporal influence in this controversially Catholic island.

At the same time this was the one place in the Empire where the British seem to have been over-awed by their environment, and by their predecessors in office. No feathered Ashanti, shogun or sultan much impressed these imperialists, whose greatest strength was a conviction of utter superiority. 'Tyrannical, drunken, debauched, cheating, intriguing, contemptible Amirs', is how Sir Charles Napier defined the bejewelled Princes of Sind. Malta's previous incumbents, however, were in a class apart. One could not sneer at the

Malta

Knights of the Order of St. John. In so many ways they behaved just as the British did themselves, and honoured similar values. Fighting spirit, a taste for splendour, the team spirit and the family tradition—all these characteristics of the Order exactly matched the British imperial ethos, and made the Knights in retrospect sound a very decent lot. 'A magnificent and munificent body of men', is how they were described by Sir Harry Luke, a late British Lieutenant-Governor of the island.

They were socially beyond cavil, too, being aristocrats not of any trumpery provincial creation, but from the great houses of European chivalry. This undoubtedly impressed the men of Empire, whose days of consequence so often ended, as Kipling cruelly wrote, when

> . . . *the Middle Classes take them back,*
> *One of ten millions plus a C.S.I.*

There was nothing ludicrous about the great floor of St. John's, laid wall to wall with the slabbed escutcheons of the Knights, glorious with helmets, scrolls and patronymics, and marvellously suggestive of inherited privilege. These were patricians worth succeeding: they were not merely grand and white (some of them indeed actually British), but soldiers and sailors too—and dead.

So for the most part, one feels, the British hardly ventured to tamper with the heritage of the Knights. Generally they adapted respectfully to it. The house of the Commander of Galleys became the house of the Dockyard Captain. The Fort of St. Angelo became H.M.S. *St. Angelo*. Where the galleys had careened the ironclads refitted, and in the palace of the Knights of Provence, who had seldom pandered to Maltese social pretensions, the committee of the Union Club scrupulously blackballed Maltese applications for membership. A British Governor sat in the Palace of the Grand Masters, where generations of soldier-priests had ruled before him, distributing the pomp of Empire in a very similar manner, and surrounding himself with the more or less sacred effigies of kings and queens of England. There was once a suggestion, wisely rejected, that one of the Knights' churches should be requisitioned for Anglican use: the narrow alley-way called Strait Street, notorious among the Knights for pleasures and skullduggery, was lustily adopted by the bravos of the Royal Navy too, and known throughout the Fleet as 'The Gut'.

Today the British in their turn have gone. The Gut looks, to my innocent eye, quite respectable. The Union Club is the National Museum. The house of the Commander of the Galleys was bombed by Britain's enemies during the last war. Only a wan rearguard keeps those flags flying over H.M.S. *St. Angelo*, and the slave quarters in the fort below, once bomb-proof stores for the Navy, are now little more than shuddery tourist attractions. This particular layer of the Maltese palimpsest—the British, that is, upon the Knightly—can best be seen now, oddly enough, right at the top: for the Palace of the Grand Masters remains the headquarters of a Governor-General, and is a lively last reminder of Malta's place in the structure of Empire.

A radio mast stands on the roof, and inside, above the arcades and hibiscus courtyards, above the clamour of the market in the Fuq il-Monti, His Excellency still presides among those royal portraits— copies mostly, of Lawrence or of Winterhalter, but sumptuously suggestive all the same of the lost imperial order. The Legislative Council meets within the Palace, too, hung about by the superb Gobelin tapestries woven for the Knights, but seated at rows of very Victorian desks. Among the heraldics of the Grand Masters are displayed the successful bids for Government tenders—ball-cocks for technical schools, steam-hammers for the dockyard: in the Armoury, beyond the splendid presecods, pauldrons and tassets of the Knights, stand the skeletonic remains of *Faith*, one of the three Gloster Gladiator fighters which created a Maltese legend in 1940.

Two lists of dignitaries are inscribed on the stately oval staircase of the palace. At the bottom are named the twenty-eight Grand Masters of the Order of St. John in Malta—Philippe Villiers de L'Isle Adam, Jean Parisot de La Valette, Ramón Perellos y Roccaful, Ferdinand von Hompesch. At the top are listed the thirty eight British Commissioners and Governors—Sir Hildebrand Oakes, Sir Henry Storks, General Sir John du Cane, or Field Marshal the Right Honourable Viscount Gort, V.C., G.C.B., C.B.E., D.S.O., M.V.O., M.C., A.D.C. to His Majesty the King.

Architecturally the British did not leave much behind. Here there are none of those glorious halls of Government, topped with pagoda or Saracenic dome, which gave an eccentrically Gothic flourish to the Raj elsewhere. There was no call in Malta for symbolic expressions of democracy, like the great Parliament buildings on the hill at Ottawa, and no need for the cool verandahed villas, phlox in the flowerbeds and banyans on the lawn, that sheltered the Governors and Admirals

Malta

of the tropics. The purposes of the British in Malta were essentially those of the Knights: what was good enough for a Grand Master was good enough for a Governor, and the harbours of Valletta and the Three Cities could hardly be more nobly fortified than they were already. Here and there, though, one may see physical traces of the imperial taste, varying in style down the generations as the ideology of Empire shifted.

Consider, for example, the Anglican Cathedral of St. Paul, splendidly situated on the shores of the Grand Harbour, and built at the order and expense of Queen Adelaide—who, visiting the colony in 1838, was shocked to discover no Anglican place of worship. The tower and spire of this fine church, experts assure us, honour an old Maltese tradition: but the spirit of the building is quintessentially English. Serenely it stands there above the harbour, placing its faith in God and the Established Church, and its simple cool interior speaks of self-control and certainty. It is built for the devotions of clean-limbed, blue-eyed administrators of Macaulayan mould, governing their subject peoples by the rules of a classical education.

The Royal Naval Hospital on Bighi, though a Maltese architect built it, looks similarly composed, standing there in such symmetrical contrast to the warlike flamboyance all around: and beside the entrance to Grand Harbour an entrancing little Grecian temple, set among the flowers of Lower Barracca Gardens, preserves the memory of Alexander Ball, the first British Governor of Malta. As Victoria's century passed, such gentle memorials of Empire became outmoded, and the British were concerned to build bigger and more showy. Now the monumental Victoria Gate was built in the flank of Valletta, a fortress-gate fit for admirals or empresses leading direct from the waterfront beneath a gigantic royal crest, skew-whiff into the heart of the stronghold. Now the Methodist Church in Floriana proclaimed in its bosomy Gothic elaboration the evangelical fervour of Empire, and Barry's monumental Opera House (bombed in the Second World War) arose beside Kingsgate to remind the Maltese of their masters' terrific wealth and lofty culture.

But it was a militant age, the age of Salvation Armies and Boys' Brigades, Jingo and G. A. Henty, and most of the rest were works of war—great sandstone barracks chiefly, in orderly echelon above the sea at St. George, or crowned with a clock-tower in a hill beside the ancient capital of Medina, as if to provide a virile riposte to its medieval reticence. From shore almost to shore in the northern part of the

Malta

island, following a geological fault, the British erected a defensive system called the Victoria Lines. This is unmistakably a prodigy of Empire. Its glowering forts, sunk beneath grassy mounds, are linked by positively Khyberian walls, and were designed to keep at bay those hereditary enemies of the British Empire, the French. Some of the bastions are now used by the Malta defence forces, but for me they are peopled still by the Lockharts, Yeatman-Biggses and Prendergasts of the imperial myth: up there in the tingling stony air of the island, spiced with herbs and soil-smells, I can still fancy the scarlet of the sentries at their watch, and catch the flash of the Maxim guns.

Malta had its moments of imperial significance in the nineteenth century—notably when Disraeli posted Indian troops there in 1878, and was accused of selling out the Empire to the barbarians. It was, though, in the period after the First World War that the island reached its imperial apogee. Politically it was a shaky time, as successive island constitutions were devised and withdrawn, and the endemic tensions of the place repeatedly erupted. Imperially it was a time of splendour. In those days the British Mediterranean fleet was the most powerful single naval formation in the world, and when the Second World War broke out, and Malta stood defiant beneath the Union Jack in the middle of *Mare Nostrum*, then the island became, for a year or two, the most honoured and heroic of all the imperial possessions.

Of this there is little to show—only scars, pill-boxes, memorials to the dead. Lordly though they looked at anchor, by the 1920s and 1930s the British had lost their imperial assurance, and were more likely to be restoring pre-Baroque village churches than building uncompromising cathedrals of their own. There was no successor to the unmistakably imperial manner of the High Victorian architecture, the late Empire-builders generally preferring mock-Georgian: Bauhaus left no mark on the Raj. Even the war memorials, once so florid or maudlin, became in the late glow of Empire a little diffident: no epic monument commemorates Malta's great days of the 1940s, and their most telling memorial is a plaque affixed to the outside of Government House—'*To Honour her brave People I award the George Cross to the Island Fortress of Malta to bear witness to a Heroism and Devotion that will long be famous in History. GEORGE R.I.*'

So if historically the Empire reached its Maltese conclusion with a marvellous bang, architecturally it went out with a whimper, ad-

mirably expressed I thought by those concrete pill-boxes one sometimes sees in the purlieus of new holiday hotels on the island, prettied
up with traditional drystone walling to look like megalithic summer-
houses. All in all, for the best evocation of the whole imperial story,
for a proper taste of its pathos, splendour and guts, one must go back
to the beginning of the British presence—before the pill-boxes, before
Victoria Gate, even before Queen Adelaide's cathedral, to the oldest
corners of the Protestant cemetery of Ta Braxia, outside the Valletta
walls. This is a gentle weedy place, knocked about in air raids and
still being extended in its outer edges, and in it you will find all the
classic phrases of the imperial epitaph, as it is inscribed on slabs and
obelisks across the world—'Fell from Aloft'. . . . 'Died at Sea About
70 miles from this Island'. . . . 'Died of the Cholera Fever'. . . .
'Erected by his Fellow-Officers in token of their Melancholy Es-
teem'. . . . Here lie in incongruous proximity William Paynter of
St. Ives, Mate of the Barque *Adam*, and Thomas Dyke Acland Fortes-
que Esquire, Captain of H.M.S. *Phoebe*: and here too is little Minnie,
four and a half years old, daughter of an evangelical Battery Sergeant-
Major—'I'M GONE TO JESUS! WILL YOU COME!!'

This is the stuff of Empire. In Ta Braxia the British presence
seems paradoxically alive, and touches us more closely than any
plume or gonfalon of dead grandee aloof upon the floor of the Co-
Cathedral.

Architecturally, it seems, the British made few converts in Malta.
The able Maltese practitioners continued to work in their own style,
and one of the more unexpected triumphs of British imperialism is
the Addolorata cemetery at Paola, which looks from a distance magnificently High Anglican, but turns out to be uncompromisingly
Catholic.

In manners and mores the imperial influence was more telling. At
home the Maltese are said to eat glorious vegetable stews, cuttle-fish
stewed in wine with nuts and raisins, eggs wrapped in slices of beef
with olives and bacon. In public they stick almost universally to *la
cuisine Anglaise* as it was in its dreariest post-war phase. Football
pools, *News of the World*, Bingo, *Coronation Street*—all play their
parts in the contemporary culture of Malta. Everywhere military
manners survive. 'As from 2000 hours', says a notice in the Malta
Hilton, 'jacket and tie will be required'. Lady Bayley and the Misses
MacDonald still do the flowers at the Anglican Cathedral, Instructor

Malta

Captain Malkin and Squadron Leader Fiddaman are among the sidesmen. Shiny as ever is the heavy brass name plate of the Malta Gas Office: empty but still in business are the bars the Navy used, The Happy Return, The Lucky Star, even the Cricketers' Arms on the shore of Marsaxlokk Bay.

Most poignantly of all, the British have left behind a legacy of loyalty. The Maltese are probably not so sentimentally anglophile as the British like to think, but they do retain a nostalgic affection for the lost Empire and its values. Many of those bars are called The Friend to All, an eponym for the grand old Sir William Dobbie, Governor of the island from 1940 to 1942. Many Maltese still appear to think that British was, on the whole, best, and when the superb ships of the United States Sixth Fleet sail into the Grand Harbour, bristling with rocketry and electronics, they are disparagingly compared to the *real* battleships of the old days. The Maltese are of mixed ethnic origins, part Arab, part Phoenician perhaps, but a century and a half of British rule has given the island an oddly northern ambience, steady and self-controlled. The traffic flows politely in Malta. The change is sure to be correct. The policemen still look remarkably like bobbies. Though the law is derived from the Roman code, and is handed down in Valletta from a vast and brand-new Classical palazzo, still the manner of its administration remains imperially familiar. The Englishman in Malta does not yet feel altogether abroad.

The Maltese also retain from the imperial connection an aura of glory. The most splendid episode in Malta's history was the second great siege, of 1940, which was the island's chief contribution to the epic of Empire. The first Great Siege, in 1565, was hardly more than a battle between feudalisms. The second was Malta's own, and there was scarcely a Maltese who did not play his part in it. In the whole story of the British Empire there was no more creditable episode— this small and distant subject people making its own heroic sacrifices in the last and most worthwhile of the imperial wars. It is easy nowadays to smile at the spit and polish of the old Fleet, the ritual splendour of Admiralty and the hierarchical pomp of Government, but never did pageantry pay off so well, or leave so brave an afterglow.

It is over now. The destroyers have gone like the galleys before them, and the Maltese remain Maltese. Their language is reviving, their own island shapes and textures are coming into fashion, and year by year

Malta

the island is returning into the comity of Europe. Soon, as the Germans, the Italians and the Scandinavians flock in, to make of this another Majorca, or a cheaper Sardinia, the British will be no more than foreigners in Malta, as detached from the monuments of their imperial past as Italian tourists in Bath. Already they are beginning to lose their proprietary air, as the imperial instincts and memories fade, and only the more elderly and Guildfordian of them pause for long before the lists of Admirals Commanding, in order to demonstrate their familiarity with the Culme-Seymours or the Fortescues.

In the end, no doubt, we shall even forget those battleships. When I was there last the only British warship in Grand Harbour, tucked away in Dockyard Creek beside the Steam Bakery, was the coastal minesweeper *Stubbington*, 360 tons. 'Stubbers', I assumed, for short.

SWAZILAND

On a weekday the dirt road from Mbabane to Piggs Peak, in Swaziland, is very quiet. An occasional car announces its approach with a plume of dust across a distant ridge. Women pass in twos or threes on their way to market. There are a few of those solitary wizened wanderers, sunk in meditation, who seem to stride perpetually across the expanse of Africa. The hills around are sparsely populated, and until one reaches the forests of the north the landscape is bare and for the most part apparently deserted.

But at the weekend, when the tourists drive in from Johannesburg, things are different. Then the road bursts raucously and inexplicably to life, and Africa performs brilliantly all along your route. Jostling vivacious boys sell wooden birds and animals. Chorus lines of infants in palm-leaf skirts suddenly burst into dance routines. Adorable naked babies scramble precariously over rocks in the middle of mountain streams, while their mothers gossip over the washing. Blind men walk with their hands held high above their heads, goatboys herd heroically bearded goats. Every sort of costume asserts itself, from the indefinably tribal, accoutred with feathers, beads and shields, to the sober-sided, mission-school, Sunday morning three-button suit.

The air seems to sizzle. Smiles gleam, hands wave, colours clash, children dance, dust billows, goats scamper, bicycles wobble, and if ever you stop for a moment, in the most isolated and abandoned corner of your route, in a flash, by the sorcery of this continent, a black boy uncurls or uproots himself from the ground, or detaches himself from a rock, or emerges from the river shallows, to come and have a look at you.

In all Africa there is no more vividly African place than Swaziland: and this sudden flaring of an entire landscape, like the magic appearance of the spring flowers when the rain falls at last, is like a spontaneous ritual of African-ness—*négritude*, as the African intellectuals say—both marvellous and perturbing to experience.

Swaziland

Perturbing not because it is unfriendly, but because it suggests to western sensibilities so many mysteries. To the innocent from another culture Africa is a half-closed book. We see only the outward signs of the inner genius—only the display that gives expression to the instinct, only the forms which have been evolved over the centuries to reflect or mask the intricacies of religion, social order and artistic sense which lie at the roots of *negritude*.

For most of us the first and simplest mystery, in the Balkanized Africa of the 1970s, is the mystery of where anywhere is. Swaziland is easier than most, first because it has never changed its name, secondly because it forms a neatly identifiable little enclave within the frontiers of the South African Republic. Until 1968 it was a British Protectorate, its African integrity jealously guarded by London against the encroachments of apartheid. Now it lives, willy-nilly, in compromise. It is an independent kingdom ruled by His Majesty Sobhuza II, with its own parliament, armed forces and diplomatic representatives: a black African State officially dedicated to the ideal of racial equality. But squeezed as it is between the Republic on three sides and Portuguese Mozambique on the fourth, it has had to come to terms with white supremacy. A customs union links it with South Africa, Swaziland getting ·53033 of the joint customs income. South African money is current in Swaziland, South Africa provides most of the tourist trade, and many South Africans, Boers and British, live in the country—my favourite Swazi address is that of H. S. Herbst, Killarney, Hhohho.

You might suppose that all this might create awkward anomalies. The powerful republic, though, looks with a fairly approving eye upon the minuscule kingdom. For private citizens of South Africa Swaziland provides not only magnificent scenery, but the more direct allures of legal gambling and accessible pornography, both verboten at home. And for the South African Government, Swaziland stands as a living example of apartheid in its loftiest sense—a separate Negro State within southern Africa, ruled by a black king along traditional tribal lines: just what, in the manifestos of the apartheid theorists, separate development is really supposed to mean.

Swaziland indeed is almost like an exhibition country, clothed in that meticulous decorum which the British brought to their possessions and protectorates everywhere. Its two principal towns, Mbabane and Manzini, are trim garden settlements, with prominent post offices and cosy places for coffee. Its central landscapes are mountainous,

Swaziland

dotted here and there with hygienic-looking kraals. Its southern regions are flat ranchlands, hot and empty, prickled with scrub. Its western reaches are covered with a particularly disciplined kind of forest—one of the largest man-made forests on earth, scrupulously categorized in blocks, and functionally centred upon a large sawmill. Swaziland is a layered, staked sort of country, logically disposed, as though it has been organized for demonstration purposes.

Consider almost any valley of central Swaziland, off the tourist routes and away from the towns, any fine morning before lunch. It is likely to offer one of those views that have no particular culmination or focal point—no foreground monument, no snowline behind—but is like a diorama in a museum, diligently filling its frame. Patches of mealie give green body to the scene, with clumps of tall reedy grass here and there, and the hills are slabbed with grey basalt, the colour and apparently the texture of elephant hide. Birds with long black floppy tails fuss about the place; dragon-flies waver over the passing stream; from the dark trees huge seed-pods hang, like sacks of bird-food.

Gently across this setting move the Swazis—at a leisurely, companionable pace, for they are not an urgent people. Two bullocks, perhaps, are hauling a sledge piled with logs, preceded by a small girl in blue carrying an axe, encouraged by a man with a huge whip of ox-hide, followed by a couple of women with enamel pots on their heads and blanketed babies on their backs. Unattended donkeys potter in their trail, infant boys supervise a goatherd on their flank, and the whole scene seems poised in time—neither modern nor archaic, neither primitive nor progressive, but simply organic, like the birds or the basalt slabs, to this particular little piece of Africa.

The Swazi heart beats bravest in the Ezulwini valley, between Mbabane and Manzini. The valley slopes away gently to the south, surveyed from either side by austerely handsome hills, and it is the shrine of everything most necessary to Swazi tradition, prosperity and self-respect—the Kyoto, Stratford-on-Avon and Las Vegas of Swaziland, all in one. Here is the Royal Swazi Hotel and Casino, for example, which contributes so lavishly to the kingdom's wealth. Here are the spanking Parliament buildings bequeathed by the British, an earnest of democratic intention though thoughtfully fitted, in their more vulnerable offices, with bullet-proof glass. Here is the office of the Swazi National Council, the headquarters of tribal authority,

Swaziland

providing a traditional counter-weight to the political parties up the road. Most important of all, here is the royal kraal of Lobamba, the ceremonial capital of the Swazi nation, which houses a few score of the King Sobhuza's unnumbered wives, and the highly influential State functionary called the Queen Mother (not the King's mother at all—in fact one of his senior wives).

The King is inescapable in his kingdom. His picture hangs in every Government office and almost every shop. His princely relatives are found in every capacity, Prime Minister to telephone operator. His royal activities fill the columns of the morning paper, and dignify the bulletins of Radio Swazi. His name or honorific is attached to schools, hotels, roads, fields of experimental agriculture. Everything is opened by him, dedicated to him, patronized by him. His power, though not absolute, is distinctly persuasive. He is, though now in his 70s, a very active and diligent ruler, and he is unquestionably the most remarkable spectacle in Swaziland.

I first saw him at the offices of the National Council, attended by a functionary called The Eye Of The King. His subjects fell on their knees, or even on their faces, as he passed, but he offered me a kindly greeting, and I looked him Jeffersonianly in the eye. I shall never forget the moment. He has the most remarkable, most twinkling, most pungent, most mischievous, altogether most entertaining face in the world. He seems to radiate an amused but a resolute complicity, as though he knows what a preposterous charade life is, but is determined to make the best of it. He was dressed that day in European clothes, as he generally is: when he wears his tribal costume, a stunning assembly of feathers, bright textiles and talismanic brooches, the impact must be terrific.

I was not deceived by the monarch's merry eye. I knew him to be an able and worldly politician, tempered by long contact with the British, educated in South Africa, well-travelled and urbane. At the same time his roots are deep in that African underworld to which I must always remain a stranger. He is only one generation removed from the days of royal smelling-outs in Swaziland, when his ferocious father King Bubu discovered his enemies by the divinations of witch-doctors, and generally had them killed. The royal kraal at Lobamba is still run on the old lines—not with witchcraft, though the art still flourishes in Swaziland, but with an unchanged devotion to the old traditions, and an almost complete rejection of western values or conveniences.

Swaziland

The men of the royal guard, who keep watch over it, are strangely uniformed in kilts and skins, and are sometimes old: quavering and suspicious sentinels, their hair waxed or buttered, carrying knob-kerries and wearing badges engraved with the king's lion symbol. They receive the foreign visitor warily, and this is perhaps wise, for I can see that the royal kraal must sometimes stir a progressive, or at least a feminist spirit in many visitors from abroad. It is a large compound of round thatched huts, surrounded by a stockade of sticks and reeds, in the centre of which, like a queen bee in her hive, the Queen Mother occupies a small masonry building. The other queens live alone, a queen to a hut, doing their own cooking. Nobody knows how many wives the King has, scattered as they are among several different kraals: when I asked a member of the bodyguard a hazed look came into his eyes as he tried unsuccessfully to compute a possible total—'in accordance with age-old traditions', as an official pamphlet discreetly puts it, 'King Sobhuza has a number of wives'.

Yet when I arrived at the kraal not one was to be seen, only a sprinkling of raggety children—'some of them the king's children', said the guide, 'some of them not'. We walked through the maze of little mud alleyways in silence. We saw the cattle kraal in which, once a year, is performed the sacred reed dance, when the maidens of Swaziland are displayed *en masse* for the royal inspection. We saw the hut in which the Queen Mother, assisted by the King, conducts the Rain Ceremony in times of drought—a hut so tremendously sacred that my companions would talk only in whispers in its proximity. We saw the tumbledown building from which a previous Queen Mother, during a period of regency, had governed the destinies of all the Swazis. But we saw no queens. It was blazing hot, lunch-time approached, and I was preparing to return disappointed to the Royal Swazi Hotel, when we saw across an open yard a solitary hunched female figure, swathed in draperies, squatting outside the door of a hut.

A small boy crouched at her side, and perhaps fifteen feet away from her one of the royal guards was standing in a half-bowed posture, exchanging some words with her. 'She is an old queen', said my interpreter. 'Nobody may approach a queen closer than that. The small boy must accompany her everywhere, even to, if you will forgive me for saying, the lavatory. No queen may ever leave the royal kraal. Once chosen to be queen she must remain in this kraal for ever. The boy may be one of the king's sons, or he may not be. Some are, some are not'.

Swaziland

I stood for a moment dazed by this flow of information, and aghast at the thought of life confinement in that hot dusty harem, and the interpreter paused for a minute too before adding a last and convincing clincher.

'All those who are the king's sons', he said, 'have very noticeable faces'.

If phenomena like these baffle the western visitor, they are prosaic enough to the Swazis, whose most difficult problem must be how to reconcile their ambitions for material progress with their reverence for tribal culture. I was not surprised to learn that the incidence of mental illness is high in the country kraals. This is partly because so many men are always at work in the Transvaal mines, leaving behind a lonely and frustrated women-folk. It is partly because of the continuing pressures of witchcraft. But it is chiefly no doubt because of the clash of old and new in this complex little country. The Swazis are related to the Zulus, and speak more or less the same language, but they seem to lack the confident fire of that formidable and ferocious people: they are gentler, more easy-going, finer-strung perhaps, and so more vulnerable to the anxieties of change.

The condition is half vivacity, half malaise, and makes for constant anomalies. I think, for instance, of a respectably dressed girl, in blouse and skirt with white shoulder bag, whom I noticed outside my window one blazing noonday. She looked like a competent shorthand-typist, and she was strolling down the pavement rather as though she was wondering whether to have a salad somewhere, or make do with a milk shake. As she approached my window, however, and entered the shade of a solitary small tree, suddenly she collapsed gently and gracefully upon the ground—in one movement removing her shoes, placing her bag beneath her head as a pillow, and casting off every suggestion of western manners. In a moment she was fast asleep, like a cat on a rug: and half an hour later, when the sun had shifted over the tree and offices were reopening after lunch, I saw her springing just as suddenly back to life—without the need to straighten her skirt or even tidy her hair, immaculate and self-composed she walked out of my sight from one life-style into the next.

Or by contrast I think of a hotel in the forest country of the north where the strictest forms of *western* traditionalism are rigidly sustained—in reaction perhaps to the insouciance with which so many young Africans switch from world to world. I arrived there after

Swaziland

dark, and stopped before I entered to breathe the ecstasy of the Swazi night—a soft astringent wind on my face, like a skin-tonic—tumultuous frog-croaks from some woodland pool—smells of pine, sawn wood and dust—urgently above my heads, flashing and winking like electronic devices, the insistent stars of Africa. All my senses were ravished, but the moment I crossed the threshold of the hotel I was returned to an all too familiar earth. Ladies Are Requested, said a sign upon the wall, Not To Wear Slacks In The Dining-Room. Parents Are Requested To Keep Their Children Quiet After Dinner. Formal was the service there, wholesome was the food, and at six in the morning inexorably down the corridor I heard the door-tap of the man with the morning tea—nearer and nearer as I lay there, like a prisoner in the condemned cell, until he entered my own room with a resolute 'Good Morning' and opened the curtains to blind me with the morning sun (but I could not go to sleep again anyway, for I knew he would be back in a few minutes for the crockery).

And I think last of the Royal Swazi Casino, where *négritude* meets materialism with a glittering vengeance. This is an exceedingly luxurious place, with its own spa (there are mineral water taps in the bedrooms), its own golf course, its continental chefs and its European croupiers—black operators, it is thought, would somehow alter the *feel* of roulette. The Royal Swazi is strong on conventions, offering a constant stream of South African business groups full conference facilities in the morning, golf in the afternoon, booze and grub in the evening and gambling all night. It is probably the best run resort complex in the whole of southern Africa, besides being the only casino south of Victoria Falls.

Yet vividly through it all stalks the genius of the country, horned and painted. Little Swazi boys scurry cheerfully around the gambling machines in the lobby. King Sobhuza II has been known to visit the tables. And the lawn-mowers are driven by men in glorious Swazi costume, perched on their seats like warriors on the move, their multi-coloured draperies flying in the wind as they chug tremendously between the croquet lawn and the fifteenth hole.

Royal people in Swaziland are buried in mountain caves, holy places shunned by ordinary Swazis as spirit-haunted. Such cave-sepulchres exist in several hills above the Ezulwini Valley, sheltering the ghosts of many royal generations—their bones for the most part long since crumbled into dust, only their charisma remaining.

Swaziland

One group is to be found in the hills a few miles south of Mbabane, near the head of the royal valley, and the European who owns the land kindly gave me permission to go and visit them. I would have to find my own way, he said. No Swazi would go near the place—it would be the worst of bad luck—all the rules were against it. But I would find it easily enough anyway. 'Just keep climbing. All the way up you'll hear the sound of a river away to your left. When you get to the spot where the sound of the river stops, then you'll be somewhere near the caves.'

I met nobody on the walk up, though I heard the chopping of an axe somewhere in the woods, and won a contest of wills with an obstructive herd of cows. Always to my left, as he had said, I heard the rush of water far below: until quite abruptly, when I had passed through the woods to the open hillside beyond, and stood there in a little rocky glade, I realized that the noise had stopped. The silence was abrupt, and disconcerting. I never felt myself in a more haunted spot. Presently I found the dark entrance of a cave in the hillside, half-blocked with rubble and brambles: and as I stood there braving the resentment of the dead I saw in my mind's eye the cortège which had once laboured up that hillside to take the royal corpse inside— the body embalmed in a black ox-hide, the head shrouded with the bladder of a black goat, the hands holding twigs from ritual shrubs— brought up here secretly on a moonless night, lying on a wooden bier, and entombed there in the cavern with a black tethered goat, never to be seen again.

On my way down I began to feel rather queer, and the next two days I spent violently ill in my bedroom. One should respect the rules, in Africa.

TROUVILLE

I had to look up Trouville on the map, but when I got there I knew it at once—not from any specific book or painting, but from a whole temper or even genre of art. There lay the long empty foreshore, with only a few shrimp catchers knee-deep in its sand pools; and there along the boardwalk strolled a group of these women that Boudin loved, blurred and shimmery in flowered cottons; and the beach was lined with a gallimaufry of villas, gabled, pinnacled or preposterously half-timbered; and three fishing boats with riding sails chugged away off-shore; and over it all, over the sands and the estuary and the distant promontory of Le Havre, there hung a soft impressionist light, summoned out of moist sunshine, high rolling clouds and the reflection of the sea. I knew the scene at once, from Monet and Bonnard and Proust. The English were the modern inventors of the salt-water resort, and made it fashionable to frequent the beaches; but the French first saw the beauty of the seaside scene, and transmuted into art all its perennial sights—the slant of that white sail, the stoop of that child beside his sand castle, the preen of the great ladies along the promenade.

This particular aesthetic was born in Trouville. It was among the earliest of the French seaside resorts, for a time it was the grandest, and at the back of our minds it is half familiar to us all.

Not far below the Seine estuary a little river called the Touques arrives unobtrusively at the English Channel, flowing through the lushly wooded landscape of Normandy, and surrounded at its mouth by a superb sandy beach. At high tide along this shore the sea rises to the very edge of the fields and orchards; at low tide an immense plateau of gold and sea shells is exposed, with chunks of black rock jutting out to sea, and a million infinitesimal crustaceans hopping about in the shallows. On the right bank of the Touques, almost at its mouth, there stood at the beginning of the nineteenth century the isolated village of Trouville—once a commercial port of some im-

155

Trouville

portance, later overtaken by better situated rivals and reduced to the status of a minor fishing station. The Channel here abounds in mackerel, eel, hake, turbot, sole and every kind of shellfish; a packet boat connected Trouville with Le Havre across the estuary; the village pottered along in picturesque modesty, with no great claim to fame, and not much hope of fortune.

In this condition the artist Charles Mozin discovered it in the 1820s. In a long series of affectionate paintings he portrayed every detail of Trouville in its pristine days: the few villas beside the sand, the horsemen plodding across the river at low tide, the brawny fisherwomen, the bright sails of the boats along the quays, the colonnaded fish market beside the water front, and above all the limpid hush that seems to have hovered over the little town. His pictures, not very distinguished examples of the romantic school, are mostly forgotten now: but they were exhibited in Paris, and they introduced the world to the charms of a coastline hitherto considered bleak, blighted and impossibly primitive. Other artists followed Mozin to Trouville, and writers too, and presently the great caravan of fashion found its way to the Normandy shore, and made the name of Trouville synonymous, for a brief but gorgeous heyday, with the pleasures of the Second Empire.

It was a full-blown sort of climax. Napoleon III's regime began brilliantly, matured lavishly, and died in humiliation. Under its aegis, all the more sumptuous arts flourished. Romanticism flounced through its rich decline. Fashion went in for ribbons, crinolines and massive flowered bonnets. Sainte-Beuve presided over a sparkling school of literary criticism, painters like Courbet and Manet were bringing a daring new splendour to realist art. Led by the Empress Eugénie, herself a creature of infinite sensuality, the Second Empire fell upon Trouville like some overwhelming rich aunt, all scent and furbelows. The boardwalk was laid upon the sands, and above it, beneath the bluffs, a parade of hotels and villas arose—very assured, very opulent, with parasols and wicker chairs on their verandas, and whirligigs on their eaves. At the point where the river reached the sands, they built a huge casino, a regular monument of a place, with opulent assembly rooms in the latest style, and carriage drives fit for any imperial barouche.

The mansions of the rich crept up the wooded hillsides. Two resplendent new churches were erected. Restaurants sprang up along the

Trouville

waterfront for those of *le beau monde* who wished to taste the adventure of dining among the fishermen. Trouville became a catalyst of the grand and the quaint. Where the fishing quay ended, the village began. The port remained a little port, but to the new resort came the Emperor himself and all of his racy, glamorous but not always very reputable court. The Empire set a seal upon Trouville, and the taste and style it engendered in this place have remained ever since part of the French artistic consciousness. Flaubert, Dumas, Victor Hugo, Boudin, Rossini, Gounod, De Musset and Dufy all felt the spell of the little town. Whistler stayed there with Courbet, Monet with Boudin, and nearly half a century after the fall of the Empire Trouville contributed its elements to the Baalbec of Marcel Proust, where the sea looked like a painted fan through the windows of La Raspelière, where Albertine and her friends of the little band idled on the boardwalk, and where the Narrator himself pursued his introspections in 'that Pandora's box, the Grand Hotel'.

So I recognized it all: the sea and the sand from the painters, the style from the history books, and the very stance of the hotel manager from the pages of *A la Recherche du Temps Perdu*. Trouville has not much grown since Proust's day—or even since Eugénie's. The countryside behind it remains delectably unspoiled, with its famous stud farms hidden away among the elms, and strong emanations of milk, fruit and rough cider. The combination of green grass and sand, meeting at the foreshore, still makes the view from the beaches feel like one of those glimpses you get from the deck of a ship, when the passing landscape seems close but altogether unattainable, as though you are seeing it through plate glass. Across the estuary Le Havre has spread down its peninsula with oil tanks and tall apartment blocks, but its very hint of power and bustle, seen distantly across the water, only heightens Trouville's sense of detachment.

History is kind to pleasure places, and Trouville has been spared by the wars. Long ago the English corsairs used to raid it, but in modern times nobody has much harmed the town. A plaque in one of the churches gratefully records the fact that the invading Prussian armies of 1871 never came farther than Honfleur, fifteen miles up the coast. In the last war, though the Allies bombed the German defences on the neighbouring hills, and fifty-six citizens of Trouville lost their lives in the Resistance—though the beaches were closed and the hotels requisitioned by the Germans—nevertheless when the liberating Belgians marched in, all was in reasonable order. Today the war

Trouville

memorial outside the Town Hall, with an urn of ashes from Buchen-
wald, is all that is left to remind us that this was enemy-occupied
territory—with one old German blockhouse beside the sands, and
the remains of the Atlantic Wall ignominiously on the heights behind.

This impunity means that Trouville, not so far along the shore
from Utah Beach or Arromanches, has a curiously preserved or
pickled air. It is a period piece, more perfect than most. Its balance of
commerce and pleasure has been scrupulously maintained, and you
can enjoy today almost the same mixture of sensations that the
courtiers and the artists enjoyed a century ago. The core of the town
remains the Casino. This has aged a little since its ceremonial opening, and has rather gone down in the world. Part of it is a cinema,
part of it a salt water spa, part a night club, part a waxwork show,
part a fire house, part a shabby kind of tenement. As an architectural
whole, nevertheless, it is still imposingly snooty, and looks faintly
exotic—like a vast Mongol marquee, perhaps, with bobbles and
domes and flagstaffs, and its own name in large and ornate letters
above the entrance.

On my first evening in Trouville I made my way to the steps of this
old prodigy and, leaning against a marble pillar, surveyed the town
before me. The square outside the Casino, dotted with trees and
used as a car park, is asymmetrical, and this splaying of its form makes
it look exactly like one of those panoramic postcards popular among
our great-grandmothers, in which several negatives were tacked together, and the view came out peculiarly elongated, smaller at the
edges than in the middle. From this distorted apex I could see both
halves of Trouville. To my left lay the beach and all it represents, the
pride, the old grandeur and the space. To my right, the fishing boats
were lined up beside the quay, bright awnings ornamented the shop
fronts, and all was cluttered intimacy. Both styles were essential, I
realized that evening, to the art form that is Trouville; and it is the
confrontation of the two, set against the light and scale of the foreshore, that gives the aesthetic of the seaside its especial tangy charm.

I looked to my right first, towards fisherman's Trouville—still as
in the 1820s, any romantic's delight. The tide was high, and the
upper works of fishing smacks lined the river boulevard—tangled
structures of rope and rigging, hung with flags, buoys, lifebelts, nets
and paintpots, and undulating slightly at their moorings. Here and
there a crew was unloading its catch in crates upon the quay, while

Trouville

the fish merchant gravely calculated the value, a huddle of housewives knowingly discussed the quality, a few tourists looked on with the glazed fascination that dead fish inspire in almost everyone, and several small boys in their blue school smocks wormed and giggled through the crowd. There were men angling, too, with heavy rods and voluminous canvas satchels. There were porters lounging around the *poissonnerie*, in stained overalls and nautical caps. High-wheeled carts were propped against walls, there was a noise of hammering from a boatyard, and the fish stalls down the street glistened with crabs, lobsters, jumpy things like big water fleas, twitching eels, clams, oysters and mackerel with a cold bluish tinge to their flanks. Fishiness was everywhere—fish smells, fish lore, fish skills, fish in boxes, fish in baskets, and mounds of shellfish (crabs embedded in mussels, lobster claws protruding from a grave of clams) upon the pavement tables of the restaurants.

For Trouville is still a working town: and behind its water front, workaday good sense fills the tight mesh of streets at the foot of the hill. There are shops that sell nets and tackle; shops lusciously flowing with the fruits, vegetables and cheeses of Normandy; trim cafés full of mirrors and tobacco smoke; a couple of big chain stores; and up in the grounds of the hospital, overgrown with ivy and embellished with archaic saintly figures, the original church of Trouville, thirteen paces long from door to altar, in whose reverent obscurity the fishing people worshipped for several centuries before the first tourist set eyes upon this place. All the stubborn variety of French provincial life stirs along those streets. Trouville is rich in tough twinkling old ladies, eccentrically dressed and wheeling their groceries on basket trolleys, and in those shabby but courteous old gentlemen of France who might be anything from dukes to retired milkmen, and wear high starched collars in the middle of August. But there are many laughing representatives of the new French generations, taller, gayer and more confident than we have ever known French people before, with beautiful children in the back seats of small family cars, and a sense of bright emancipation from a fusty past—figures from that rich young France which is, as D. W. Brogan has observed, 'something that Europe and the world have not seen for a century'.

Fisherman's Trouville is never torpid. It admirably illustrates those aspects of the French genius which are unalterably organic—close always to the earth, the sea, the marriage bed and the neigh-

Trouville

bour's gossip. The Duchesse de Guermantes, the ineffably aristocratic chatelaine of Proust's great novel, loved to tell country anecdotes in a rustic accent: and it is this ancient attachment to earthy things, so vital a part of the French artistic energy, that the right-hand view from the Casino best expresses.

Then I looked to the left, and there lay another France in esplanade. Exuberantly the hotels and villas clustered about the beach—none of them young indeed, but all of them gay, like jolly old gentle folk, in lace and grey toppers, out to enjoy themselves. It was an elaborate age that made Trouville famous, and the buildings of this resort are flamboyantly individualist. Some are gloriously encrusted with coils, domes and flourishes of classicism. Some are expensively faced in Normandy halftimber, and stand incongruously beside the sands like farmhouses on Fifth Avenue. Others go to wilder excess, and are built like castles, like fairy palaces, even in one case like a Persian caravanserai. The rooftops of this Trouville are punctuated with golden birds, pineapples, crescent moons, spindles, metal flowers and urns, and all the way up the hillside among the trees the mansions stand in majesty, unabashed by shifts of taste or society, and still looking, behind their ornamental gates and protective shady gardens, almost voluptuously comfortable.

Not much has changed since the great days of the resort. The bright little tents that people put up on the beach are made of nylon nowadays, but with their suggestion of eastern dalliance still recall the enthusiasms of Delacroix or Gautier. Cars are not admitted to the beach, so that the long-celebrated boardwalk, however crowded it becomes in high summer, is still quiet and leisurely. Nobody has erected a skyscraper hotel, or built a bowling alley, and severe instructions affixed to flagstaffs govern the decorum of the sands. The miniature golf course, beside the Casino, is a very model of genteel entertainment, admirably suited to the inhibitions of elastic-side boots and bustles: with its painted wooden windmill for knocking balls through, its tricky inclines and whimsical hazards, it seems to ring perpetually with the silvery laugh of ladies-in-waiting, and the indulgent banter of colonels. As for the unexploded mines and bombs which occasionally turn up along these shores, Trouville officially classifies them as '*Objets Bizarres*'— and what a fine old-school sniff infuses those fastidious syllables!

The Second Empire was scarcely an empire really, but it loved the

Trouville

imperial trappings, and stamped the grand manner upon Trouville. Two nineteenth-century churches overshadow the little fishermen's chapel, and are full of superior memories. In one, a large but indistinct painting has nothing to indicate either its subject or its artist, but only a plaque to tell us loftily: '*Presented by the Emperor*'. In the other stands an altar given by the Comte d'Hautpool and his wife the Princesse de Wagram—Napoleonic titles which, for all their splendour, remind us that the ruling class of this extravagant period was never quite the real thing, but rested upon the pedigree of a Corsican adventurer. The florid style of the Empire is everywhere in Trouville, and when the regime collapsed with the defeat of Napoleon III at the Battle of Sedan, the great days of the resort ended too. It was here that the fiery Eugénie stepped aboard an English yacht and sailed away into exile: and there is a sad irony to the fact that the votive plaque rendering thanks for the sparing of Trouville in that disastrous war is addressed to Our Lady of Victories.

Finally I walked behind the great mass of the Casino (looking, as the evening drew on, just as humped and portentous as Bonnard had painted it fifty years before) and across the narrow river, I saw another, larger, more glittering city on the other side. The Duc de Morny, half-brother of the Emperor himself, was paradoxically the originator of Trouville's decline. In the 1860s this enterprising speculator cast *his* eye across the Touques, and saw that the sand on the other side was just as golden, the climate just as sparkling, the sea the same stimulating sea—and the landscape entirely empty. Trouville had reached its peak of fashion; the Parisian elite was beginning to hanker for somewhere more exclusive; in a few years, upon the impetus of the duke, there arose on the left bank of the Touques the excruciatingly posh resort of Deauville.

Today it is the smartest watering place in northern France, and it looked to me that evening, from the backside of Trouville's Casino, like a vision of another age. Its clientele nowadays is richer and more cosmopolitan than Trouville's. Its casino has a turnover twice as great. Its street lights come on fifteen minutes earlier. Its race meeting is one of the most important in Europe. No fishermen's cafés soil its elegant promenades, and only yachts and speedboats sail into its basin. It is all resort. Today, if you want to explain where Trouville stands, you can best say that it's over the bridge from Deauville.

So there is a certain pathos to the prospect from the Casino at Trou-

Trouville

ville—but pathos of a gentle, amused kind. Trouville does not feel humiliated. It is this small town that the artists loved, its image, variously interpreted down the generations, that has entered all our sensibilities—Trouville's sands and sails we all dimly recognize, Trouville's ludicrous mansions that ornament the album pages, Trouville's bright light that gleams so often, with a tang of Channel air, from the walls of so many galleries. In Trouville the sun, the sea, the fishing folk and the high society became an inspiration, and created a tradition of art.

So I did not mope that evening. I crossed the square to my hotel, accepted the bows of Proust's page boys, left a note inviting Whistler and De Musset to join me for a drink at *Les Vapeurs*, and asked the maid to clean my best shoes, in case I bumped into the Empress at the Casino after dinner.

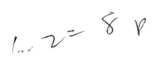

WALES

etween 8,000 cheering people, to the strains of a patriotic march, a champion strides through a gigantic pavilion, triumphant. He wears a blue robe and is escorted by flamboyant sages, and as he passes beneath the heraldic banners he waves and smiles to left and right, the great assembly rising to its feet as he passes, the music thundering around him.

He is not a conqueror home from the wars. He is not a Brazilian footballer. He is not even a pop star or a president. He is a Welsh poet, honoured by the literary establishment of his nation for the composition of a traditional ode, and now given the public recognition that this most sensuous of peoples reserves for its bards, its singers and its tellers of tales.

The Welsh, living overshadowed on the western flank of England, have preserved their nationality through art, though the literature of their ancient Celtic tongue, still the first language of some 650,000 Welshmen, and through their peculiar gift for music and histrionics, expressed both in traditional forms of chaste sublety and in the ripe romanticism that is the mode of performance wherever ordinary Welshmen meet to sing. Politically suppressed for several centuries, the Welsh enshrined their pride of race in books, music and rhetoric. Their language, given a new stamina by the nonconformist movements of the eighteenth and nineteenth centuries, became the focus of every national purpose, and one of the most important events of Welsh life was the literary and musical festival called the *eisteddfod*. Every village had its own *eisteddfod*, and rooted deep in the national awareness was the tradition of artistic contest, sponsored in antiquity by the cultivated princes of independent Wales, with their court poets and their honoured harpists, their standard rules of prosody and their happy assemblies of bards.

The village festivals were sometimes comic and sometimes pathetic, but they helped to keep Welshness alive, giving Welsh people of all classes a pride in their own artistic tradition; and since 1858 they

have come to a head in a grand Royal National Eisteddfod, which is held each year in a different Welsh town, attended by pageantry, affection, and a certain amount of slosh, and known to Welshmen all over the world as the supreme event of the Welsh calendar. It is at this famous and extraordinary festival that the poetic champions of the nation, their winning compositions selected by an academy of eminent colleagues, progress in such voluptuous glory towards their bardic chairs, to the diapason of the organ and the whirr of the television cameras from the gantries high above.

I went to the National one year at Bala, a little market town (population 2,000) on a lake in North Wales, surrounded at a proper distance by wild moorland but embedded in comfortable pasture and frequented by anglers. For a week this was the true capital of Wales and of Welsh patriots everywhere. The inns of the town were crammed; the trombones of practising brass bands sounded in the morning, the orations of pub rhetoricians at night; and over the bridge at the end of the main street there appeared in a field a bannered city of tents, booths and fluttering pavilions.

Here the essence of a nation was concentrated, just for a week, in an ambiance generally genial, but perceptibly flecked with the fanatic. Perhaps the nearest equivalent in the western world would be a gathering of Basques, another people up in arms against uniformity, and as you wander around the Eisteddfod ground you may feel in every corner the fascination of a historical anomaly. Here are the stalls of the Welsh booksellers, offering the whole range of vernacular literature, comic strip to Methodist thesis, wild nationalist denunciations and histories of the wool industry in Merioneth. Here the rival television services, state and private enterprise, diplomatically flaunt their Welshness with red dragons and Celtic charm. The London Welsh Association displays a picture gallery of eminent Welsh exiles. The Roma House Hotel in Bloomsbury promises a proper Welsh welcome for visitors to the metropolis (its manager is described as Talfryn Phillips, Tenor) and Evan Evans the sightseeing people offer Welsh-speaking guides to St. Paul's or the Tower of London.

Bearded youths of angry aspect are enrolling new members (looking gallant but sheepish, like recruits to Kitchener's New Army in ancient newsreels) to the Welsh Language Society, a fierce fraternity which agitates for the legal use of Welsh on every public occasion,

Wales

Parliament to parking meter. *Yr Enfys*, 'the journal of the Welsh people outside Wales', reports (in Welsh) the doings of the Welsh communities in Adelaide and Seattle. Argentine Airlines advertises a direct route between Wales and the Welsh settlements of Patagonia. Glorious girls in a kind of mod Welsh national costume accost you breathily with programmes outside the Wales Theatre Company pavilion, and in the centre of everything stands the grand hall, where the big ceremonies of the week are staged—the biggest movable pavilion in the world, they say, which is carted from site to site each year and looks rather like an airship hangar. The whole concourse has a medieval manner to it: and after the first rain of the week, when its grass is churned into mud rather, its duckboards squelch and its open spaces are smothered in layers of straw, it begins to look like a tournament camp of chivalric times, where knights might meet for jousting, and minstrels pluck away at madrigals.

But everything is Welsh. The English language is scarcely heard, except on the portable translation devices lent free to visitors, and every sign around you is in Welsh, from *Dim Ysmygu* (No Smoking) to *Ysgrifennydd Cyffredinol* (General Secretary). Through the turnstiles about 20,000 Welshmen pass each day, greeting old friends, shying off old enemies, following the familiar procedures of the Eisteddfod with loving concentration, knowingly assessing the chances of the Mid-Rhondda Silver Band or the Cwm-bach United Male Voice Choir, and giving the occasion a strong family flavour.

They form a courteous but not urbane assembly—sturdy country people mostly, fresh-faced and stocky, the women often of a beautiful symmetry of face and sweetness of expression, the men in down-to-earth tweedy suits and cloth caps. There is a jazzy sprinkling of mini-skirts and crimson shirts, but on the whole it looks more like the crowd at an agricultural show than an artistic attendance; for art in Wales is a social force, and if all these people are united in Welshness, they are linked too by a technical understanding, incomprehensible to foreigners, of bardic lore and standards.

For odd things happen, to foreign minds and ears, within the sanctuary of that great pavilion. Let us eavesdrop on the ceremony called the Crowning of the Bard, a climactic function of the Eisteddfod, at which the judges reward the best writer of a *pryddest*, an ode in free metres. This year, for the second time in living memory, the crown goes to a woman, for a poem about comparative religions. If we peer out of the wings on to the immense stage we may see her sitting on a throne in the middle, her crown precariously balanced on her hair-do. She looks very nice, but around her a weird company of celebrants is paraded. There are barefoot children dressed as elves, clutching bouquets and sometimes breaking into a woodland measure. There are trumpeters in velvet gowns, and harpists, and massed ranks of men and women in voluminous robes, white, green and blue, with droopy headdresses flowing around their ears and spectacles. A matron presides over a horn of plenty, a maiden cherishes a sheaf of corn, and at the front of the stage sits a group of vaguely sacerdotal figures, resplendent in medallions and breastplates, one with a banner mystically inscribed, one with an enormous sword, one with an oaken wand, some in great signet rings, some with laurel leaves upon their headdresses. Arcane symbolisms are being fulfilled up there. The sword is half-drawn from its sheath and slammed shut to a cry of *Heddwch!*—'peace!' The trumpets are blown north, south, east and west. The horn of plenty and the sheaf of corn are proffered with elfin gestures. All is done to a ritual pace, rather like a bullfight in Spain, every gesture familiar to the vast audience, every nuance understood.

This skimble-skamble jubilee is not very old—it was first ordered by an inventive Glamorgan stonemason in 1791, when romantic fancies were all the rage—but it is dear to the hearts of Eisteddfod-goers, and it suitably celebrates the part played in the Welsh survival by the academy of bards, the Gorsedd. This organization, a mystery to Englishmen, virtually runs the National Eisteddfod. With its trappings of cult and hierarchy, it has something in common with judo, and more with Masonry, and plays an unexpectedly prominent part in the everyday affairs of Wales.

Its two lowest orders (Green Robe and Blue Robe) are entered generally by examination, its highest (White Robe) is an honour reserved for distinguished artists and men of the world, many of whom have made their names outside Wales but still consider themselves Welshmen first. The Gorsedd mummeries are allegedly based upon druidical rituals, convenient precedents about which nobody really knows anything whatsoever, and the head of the order is called the Archdruid—an eminent poet elected by his peers for three years. There is a Deputy Archdruid too, and an Attendant Druid, and members of the Gorsedd adopt bardic names like the poets of old— names of mountains, or abstract qualities, or mythological heroes, by which they sometimes become so well known that the public almost forgets their patronymics, and one reads of them attending weddings or opening fêtes in their bardic capacities.

It sounds rather silly in the theory, and it looks rather comic on the stage, but it has long since become part of the Welsh folklore, so that Welshmen follow its absurdities with a sentimental indulgence, like racegoers at the Kentucky Derby, or cynical Socialists singing the *Internationale*. Actors, statesmen, great surgeons and judges are proud to put on the white robe in the Eisteddfod robing room: and there *is* something moving to the spectacle of them all up there, sharing the charade with such infectious delight, the cuffs of their pinstripe trousers showing beneath their togas.

Outside one tent three men are lost in thought, each with a pencil and a notebook. Sometimes they walk anxiously up and down, sometimes they slap their foreheads in despair, and sometimes with a muffled cry they scribble something down. They are poets extemporizing to a set theme, and in a moment or two they must go inside the tent to deliver their lines before a critical audience of aficionados, from whom one may presently hear groans, guffaws or cries of adulation. It is like a courtly contest in a tapestry, with saga-writers strumming off epics to edify princes.

The Welsh culture is a pungent abstraction, shared only by Bretons, Cornishmen and miscellaneous Gaels, and often striking observers from sharper-edged societies as unnecessarily obscure. Halfway through the Eisteddfod the prize poems are published, together with the adjudications, and when the booklet first goes on sale in the field you may see groups of men and women huddled over its pages, analysing its prosodies and disputing its verdicts. The mechanics of language are exceedingly important to the Welsh. They are an allusive people, and it is a rash foreigner who invites a really fervent litterateur to explain the inner subtleties of a poetic line— 'no, but that is not precisely it, you see, the word has another meaning too, it can have a figurative sense also—something less precise, you see—Will, come here now, how would you explain to this gentleman the exact significance in this context of *arweinydd* . . .?'

Almost nothing is crystalline. A haze seems to hang over the Eisteddfod, only partly emanating from the rain which, one day or another in any Welsh week, is almost sure to fall. The pseudo-Masonic postures are apt enough, for there is a certain secrecy to the national spirit of the Welsh, something that does not invite too facile an interpretation, but leaves its observers half-guessing. There is a kind of song to the harp, very popular at the Eisteddfod, which perfectly expresses this obscurity. The *canu penillion* is a duet for the harp and voice in which the two performers work at odds, air and descant pursuing an almost unrelated course, rhythmically, harmonically, melodically and sometimes even stylistically, until in the final phrase both streams are exquisitely united. It is, for the uninitiated, a traumatic kind of music: but then the Welsh can be, to outsiders, a disturbing kind of people.

Salt is a little short, at the National Eisteddfod. There was some mildly satiric theatre this year (exposing audiences for the first time, the papers reported, 'to bare-legged girls'), and there were experimental literary discussions, at which judges were cross-questioned about their decisions. In general, though, it is essentially a kindly gathering, cheerfully on the brink, as Welsh affairs so often are, of sentimentality. The Welsh have survived by self-regard, by convincing themselves, if nobody else, that their culture is worth preserving: self-criticism is not their *forte*, and only a few unrepentant cosmopolitans continue to suggest that standards might be higher at the Eisteddfod if some entries were allowed in English.

So for me two of the more emotional events of the Bala Eisteddfod best characterize the festival and all it represents. The first is the Welcome to the Welsh from Overseas—a frank invitation to nostalgic self-indulgence. There the returned emigrants sit on the stage of the pavilion, craggy old Australian ladies and fidgety children in T-shirts—a millionaire from Bogota, a nuclear scientist from Switzerland, New Zealanders, Canadians, Americans—envoys of the Welsh diaspora, united in heady ecstasy as the grand old Welsh anthems flood through the hall, a vibrato in every voice, a tear in every other eye.

And better still, for the proper throb of Welshness—what they call its *hwyl*, a combination of fervour and showmanship—are the contents for the male choirs. How passionately they sing, the solitary lady pianist quivering with tension, the thin Welsh faces aflame! How superbly those village Toscaninis lead their choruses—one with all the Latin flamboyance of the South Wales valleys, the next with the patrician austerity of the north! Nowhere on earth, I swear, is there an audience more minutely attentive to every demi-semi-quaver. Nowhere do such shock waves of sheer physical excitement eddy from a concert platform, measurable not so much in decibels as in calories, or perhaps horsepower.

Wales

This is the year's apex of Welshness. The Welsh will not be quite so Welsh again until the props go up next year, the druids look out their regalia again, and the next National Eisteddfod marks another year passed in the long and indomitable history of Wales. After the male voice choir contests, one of the adjudicators, in a long and elaborate address, announces and explains the judges' verdict. His speech is broadcast over loud-speakers, and throughout the Eisteddfod ground, in the drizzle of the early evening, men stand listening with grave concentration, their hands plunged in their coat pockets, weighing each sentence as though the fate of a nation depends upon its syllables.

And so, in a sense, it does.

WYOMING

I had long missed, like everyone else, the American innocence. When I first went to the States, in the 1950s, it flourished still in Norman Rockwell's world of sundae, prom, and *Saturday Evening Post*; it flickered momentarily, I think, in the successive debuts of beats, hippies, flower people and Jesus freaks; but for myself I had lately only felt its presence, and fitfully even then, among the harbourmen of New York City, in whose company, on tugs and pilot boats, flats and oil barges, I had been making some agreeable excursions. It

Wyoming

was one of these men, lounging on one side of his pilot-house while I ate a bar of Hershey's Tropical Chocolate on the other, who reproached me for despondency. 'Look, why belly-ache? If ya don't like the city, go some place else. This place ain't everywhere. We can't help it. We grew up this way. Get out of the place. Go to the Rockies or some place—but like I say, don't belly-ache. . . .'

I cherished his advice, and when the opportunity arose I booked a ticket to Wyoming, hoping to find in that remote hinterland something real in America still: for I had seen, in a statistical chart about the origins of celebrated movie actors, that while twenty-three of the most famous had been born in New York State, and fifteen in Michigan, and eleven in California, the only State in the Union unable to claim a single star was The Equality State (whose population is rather smaller than Coventry's, and whose area is rather larger than the entire United Kingdom's).

I had reached the conclusion that the downfall of the Americans had been insincerity. This is of course no news to old-school British sceptics, who have been saying for 200 years that Americans can't be trusted. But it was not exactly dishonesty that I found so inescapable in the America of the 1970s, nor even hypocrisy: it was that loss of innocence. It was a habit of deception so ingrained, so universal it seemed, that the Americans did not notice it in themselves. It was a national frame of mind. The pioneers had doubtless invented the false fraternity of American merely in order to survive. The American need to be loved was originally a withdrawal symptom of revolution. Capitalism had made the Republic itself a kind of advertising campaign. And all these elements had lately been compounded by the illusory quality of life in modern America: the combined hallucinogens of drugs, of electronics, of racial dogma, of political corruption and persiflage, which had whittled away at reality and made everything suspect, whether it be an interview with a bank manager or an argument for the preservation of Alaskan wilderness.

A worldly American friend of mine, when I told him what the tugboat man had suggested, assured me that if anything the American delusion was less profound than its British equivalent. If you stripped an Englishman of his veneer you eventually reached a core of infinite complexity: but beneath the American layers there survived, he swore, more shy by far than any English inhibitions, yearning, ancient, unfulfilled, a purity unsuspected. 'Pure white', he thought, 'virgin white at the centre.' I could only say that very different colours showed: introspective purples, crooked reds, greens for envy and acquisitiveness, black for urban crime, and a muddy, greeny, yellowy mish-mash colour for all that anxious groping, doped with hash and addled with psychiatry, with which young America stumbles pitiably towards nowhere in particular.

'But go by all means', my friend fastidiously added, 'if the West attracts you': and so I rented myself a car in Denver, a city all agog, as it happened, with newspaper revelations about downtown pornography, and drove across the State line into Wyoming. I stopped for a coffee and a salad on the way north, and the women at the counter showed me with a mock-shudder a headline in one of the local newspapers that day. I found it encouraging, on the whole. 'TEN MORE BALD EAGLES', it said, 'FOUND POISONED IN WYOMING PITS.'

'Cheyenne, our State capital', the tourist lady told me educationally, 'is essentially a railroad city, but I don't suppose, dear, railroads interest you.' There she was wrong. My images of the American naivety were inextricably linked with railroads. I had never thought the Pilgrim Fathers innocent, let alone Washington or Jefferson, and the kind of simplicity I coveted dates, I think, from the days of the Western expansion. While the patrons of American railroads were seldom childlike, the men who made and ran them do seem to have been, by our fallible standards, a genuine, rough-and-tumble lot of people, and the American railway mystique has always been a benevolent abstraction. It evokes sentimental nostalgia, a weakness I enjoy. Even now, I am told, hobos and hitch-hikers are kindly treated by the railroad men, as their tradition demands, and hardly a freight train passes in the West without a few unauthorized riders behind its steel doors.

It is true that Cheyenne is a railroad town still. One hears the wail at night sometimes, as the Irish might say, and the main downtown street demonstrates its origins by running parallel with the Union Pacific track, which pre-dated it. Everyone told me with pride that Cheyenne had been frightfully sinful in its youth, when the mobile camp of construction workers ('Hell on Wheels') reached this site with the advancing rails. Even by railroading standards, they said, it had been a wild town, with its perilous saloons and its brazen brothels, its hordes of speculators and promoters, its gunmen, its hunters and trappers, its opportunist lawyers and its tented thousands of Chinese and Irish labourers. The Civil War had just ended then, and America

Wyoming

was in a violent mood. By 1869 Cheyenne was ambitiously described as 'the gambling centre of the world', and during the same year its unofficial committee of vigilantes, administering the justice of the frontier, executed at least a dozen offenders.

'Oh', said the lady in mild surprise, 'in that case you must go and see our reconstruction of Hell on Wheels, with the locomotive, *Big Boy* . . . Authentic Relic', she continued, relapsing into her brochure voice, 'of the Railroad Era'. But it was a sorry reflection, I thought, of those rumbustious origins. Hell on Wheels turned out to be a folksy enclave of novelty shops and sideshows, surrounded by canvas awnings and closed anyway for the season. *Big Boy* was the biggest railway engine ever built anywhere, a vast black mechanism with nineteen wheels on each side: but it stood forlornly on a petty line of track in a park, Hell on Wheels flapping depressingly behind, and seemed so absolutely of the museum or the Rotary Club that I could scarcely conceive those pistons ever pumping, still less hear a cuss from its cab.

So I proceeded to the Union Pacific station itself, at 16th and Central, for nearly a century one of the main depots on the transcontinental run, where the Denver Pacific and the Colorado Central met the great U.P.R.R.—'travellers will here take a dinner', says my *Trans-Continental Railroad Guide* (1881), 'in comfortable style at one of the best kept hotels between the two oceans'. Alas, as a citadel of the old values it too lacked conviction. It seemed to be on its last legs. Trains *did* come, they told me, but they took a lot of hanging around for. The station was officially open from 10 to 5, and still possessed an office magically inscribed 'Special Agent', and housed the last of the overland stage coaches from Julesburg, Co., propped outside the ticket booths: but its mahogany fittings badly needed love and feather dusters, and so silent were the tracks, so endlessly into the distance did the lines of the Union Pacific extend in absolute hushed desertion, so utterly absent were porters, trollies, mailbags or homing pigeons in wicker baskets, that it looked to me as though never again would a train hiss to a halt at Cheyenne, to disgorge from its high steps that nervous, gauche and lovely girl to whose inevitable arrival the late-nightmovies long ago forewarned us.

But there was life of a sort outside the platforms. In line at one of the ticket windows a shabby line of men waited, standing first on one leg, then on the other, sometimes removing their Stetsons to scratch the tops of their balding heads, or passing coffee around in squashy

plastic cups. These were the redundant of the railroad. 'They'll
never close the track, never, for the freight, see, but in the meantime
here's some of the boys without a job.' The boys politely made way
for me as I edged to the head of their queue to peer through the
ticket-window: and what I saw behind was curiously disillusioning.
It is true that one man wore an eye-shade, like the telegraph operators
of old, but in most respects the scene back there, in the private
quarters of Cheyenne depot, looked less Western than Oriental. It
reminded me of Madras. It was a cameo of officialdom, framed in
dockets, files, chits in triplicate. It looked old and tired. Everybody
looked up when I appeared at the window, and offered me *babu*
smiles. 'Anything I can do for you? You looking for someone?' But
it was not what I was hoping for, the innocence was absent, so I
shook my head sadly and drove out of town.

I went to the Indian country, but soon got tired of Indians. 'I am
tired of Indians', said I to the kindly cicerone who showed me round
the Bradford Brinton Memorial Ranch House, near Sheridan, fearing
she might draw my attention to yet more portraits of squaws or
shamans, pre-Raphaelite impressions of tepee ceremonials, or (worst
of all) bead artifacts. She looked startled. It was not, I think, the
opinion that perturbed her, it was simply its expression. European
visitors to the West are not generally tired of Indians, and American
visitors would not dream of saying so.

   Part of the unreality of America, it seemed to me, was its retro-
active conscience. Americans suffered allegedly lacerating pangs
about matters they could not mend, and for which they were blame-
less anyway, and their guilt over the fate of the Indians was the prime
example. It was doubly false. For one thing no living American was
conceivably to blame, and for another the Americans did not really
feel guilty in an actual or personal way, but merely found it morally
or perhaps ecologically fashionable to appear so. Integral to the
American innocence had been a guileless violence, generally accept-
able by the morality of the time, and its denial now was part of the
national lie. How could the Americans feel guilt about the fate of the
Sioux or the Modocs? I certainly did not feel in the least guilty about
Amritsar, say, being unthought of at the time, never having heard of
the massacre until twenty-five years after the event, and possessing
neither the inclination nor the technique to massacre anybody anywhere.

Wyoming

This particular American indulgence struck me as especially sickly in Wyoming, where I did not doubt the persecution of the Indians would be continuing still, were it not for the fact that the white people, from the wickedest rich landowners to the liliest academic progressives, were no longer troubled by them. For in this State the theme, vocabulary, and flavour of the Indian presence cannot be evaded. I went to Greybull, which commemorates an old grey buffalo of Indian legend, and Crowheart, which remembers Chief Washahue of the Shoshones, dying there with a Crow warrior's heart upon his spear, and Spotted Horse, and Medicine Bow, and Ten Sleep; and I inspected the reconstructed buildings of Fort Laramie, white and spanking in the sunshine, once the storied Army headquarters of the Indian wars, now so aggressively repentant that even the wild creatures within its perimeter are officially protected, and the moment I entered its central enclosure an impertinent rabbit sprang at me.

There were memories of those wars everywhere, for Americans to tear their hair and beat their breasts over. Some I found very moving. I had never heard, for instance, of the Fetterman Massacre, but I felt I understood its import when, driving down the empty road between Sheridan and Buffalo, I saw its commemorative obelisk upon a ridge. Here the impulsive Colonel Fetterman, contemptuous of Indian tactics, led his force of seventy-nine soldiers from Fort Phil Kearney to escort a wagon-train of timber from the hills. On this grand bare windswept ridge, just before Christmas 1866, with the savage Big Horn Mountains splendidly to the east, and the wide plateau of the Wind River extending southwards snow-white and bitter—on this spot his column was ambushed, so the obelisk told me, 'by an overwhelming force of Sioux under the command of Red Cloud'. 1866! In New York in 1866, they started to build Brooklyn Bridge. In England, in 1866, Newman published the *Dream of Gerontius*. In Brisbane, in 1866, they first lit the General Post Office with gas lamps. But in Wyoming, on 21 December, 1866, Red Cloud fell upon the 18th United States Infantry, and there were no survivors.

All over Wyoming I was reminded of those old adventures, by cryptic memorials, the names of old forts, the sites of old battlefields —the Wagon Box Fight in Big Piney Creek, the Crazy Woman Fight in Johnson County, or the Dull Knife Battle of 1876, from whose carnage the surviving Cheyenne Indians, their wounds staining the snow, crept half-naked across the hills to seek refuge with Crazy

Wyoming

Horse. But the Wyoming Indians of today are a distinctly unexciting people. In the pamphlets I was shown in Cheyenne they were dressed up for festival, feathered, gaudy, bold, with horses and pipes and painted tepees. Off-duty, so to speak, they proved less virile, and seemed to me an argument less for the advantages of peace than for the stimulants of war: for it was not of course the U.S. Cavalry who destroyed the Indians, but the peacemakers, the improvers or rationalists of their day, the nineteenth-century ecologists, who herded them logically into reservations, and put the fire out.

There is only one reservation in Wyoming, the Wind River. I visited the Shoshones and Arapahoes there, vaguely hoping to find, I think, that those long-defeated tribes might be the custodians of an older relationship between man and nature, and that one day they would, like the possessors of some royal strain or talisman, emerge into their own again. But if they possessed the old panaceas, one would not know it. The Wind River Indians are taciturn, not to say surly, representatives of the old race. Even one of their own white officials admitted to me that he found them heavy going—especially, he hastily added, lest I should think him racialist, after a few years among the perfectly charming Navajos of the south. There is a large café and community hall at Fort Washakie, the agency headquarters, and I went for a cup of coffee there hoping to enjoy an informative chat with the girls at the counter. But they were not a chatty crew. Expressionless they served me, desultorily they exchanged monosyllables with their Indian customers, more bigoted than ever did I leave their reservation, vowing I would buy not another basket-work bag, admire no more antique pictographs, express no further interest in a folk-ceremony, nor ask one more diplomatic question about the communal collection of huckleberries so long as I remained in the State of Wyoming—whose motto, by the way, is Equal Rights, and whose State Flower is the Indian Paint Brush—*A strange little flower*, as Addie Viola Hudson has put it, *with a sun-kissed nose,*

> *Without any perfume, yet red as a rose.*
> *Did some Indian maiden plant you here*
> *Or are you the symbol of blood that was shed*
> *In the footprint left by the hoof of a deer,*
> *In the feud of the white man, and the red?*

Nor at first was I much beguiled by the Old Western evocations of the State. Wyoming has been a tourist trap almost since the first

Wyoming

pioneers passed this way. Among the earliest travellers in these parts were Major Sir Rose Price and Mr. William S. Baillie-Grohman, sportsmen from England, and even in the roughest days of Hell on Wheels and the Cattle Barons, dudes found their way here to shoot their buffalo and write their travel memoirs. By now history, myth, reality and tourist exploitation are inextricably confused, and at first I thought that even here, in these half-empty landscapes, in these snug ranching towns, along these terrific treeless highways, the corrosion of fraud was inescapable.

There is a lot of sham. There are silly tourist ranches, and phoney saddlers, and ghost towns preposterously resurrected, and ludicrous Wild West enthusiasms, like the collection of old Burnham's Beef, Wine, and Iron bottles. The Old West breeds its own degradations, and Wyoming often parodies itself not merely for the tourists, but for itself. I winced each time I heard the phrase Old Timer, and hurried sickened and distraught from the well-known Wyoming spectacle called the Wild Life Exhibit, which turned out to be a revolting assemblage of 100 stuffed animals and 600 sets of antlers, slaughtered personally by Mr. Dale Warren of Dubois—'*Kids* [as his publicity says] *Just Love our Baby Fawn, Baby Bear and Baby Seal*', all unhappily murdered young.

Aesthetically the memory of the Old West can be distressing, in garish water-colour or mawkish ode:

> *Out where the handclasp's a little stronger,*
> *Out where the smile dwells a little longer,*
> *That's where the West begins . . .*

while the public humour of Wyoming might be described in architectural terms as Rustic Commercial:

> *Grab the Tab*
> *Pay the Tariff*
> *Come Back Soon*
> *Or We'll Send the Sheriff*

Wyoming is a great place, too, for slogans: *The Can Do Country—Stop Roaming, Try Wyoming—Healthy, Wealthy, Growing Wyoming—Wonderful Wyoming*. Since 1936 Wyoming car number-plates have carried a publicity picture of a bucking bronco, with a whooping cowboy up, and this is far more telling an insignia of the State than the Great Seal with its scrolls and banners, or even the State Flag with its somnolent buffalo.

The patron saint of tourist Wyoming, or perhaps the managing director, is Buffalo Bill, Colonel Cody. I got very tired of him, too. He was the original hallucinogenic American, for what was genuine in him and what was pretence seems to have been unresolvable. The house where he was born is at Cody, in the north-west of the State, but that celebrated town, now a shrine to his memory, was not in fact his place of birth. It seems that in 1895 a few speculators thought of founding a new town in Wyoming. 'Horace and I had a talk, and we concluded that as Buffalo Bill Cody was probably the best advertised man in the world, we might organize a company and make him president. . . .' Colonel Cody not only agreed, but suggested that the town should actually be named after him. 'This did no harm to us, and it highly pleased the colonel.'

To clinch the arrangement Cody's birthplace was brought there from Iowa, and instantly Cody, Wyoming, became a prosperous tourist destination. It was probably the first municipality to capitalize the Western legend, which thus co-existed there in fantasy and in fact, and it has thrived ever since. A vast, emotional, and rather beautiful statue of the colonel dominates the town; he is pointing the way ahead with his rifle, leaning in his saddle to encourage the timid pioneers out of sight behind, while his horse, heroically neighing (it was modelled from life in Manhattan), raises its left fore-foot in a graceful and fortunately symmetrical pose. There is an enormous Buffalo Bill Museum, a Vatican of the Western ethos, and diverse lesser monuments to the Colonel flourish, like the Irma Hotel he built for his daughter Irma, and the Cody Stampede on Independence Day, and Buffalo Bill Day on 26 February, and Buffalo Bill souvenir counters, and Buffalo Bill coffee shops, and Buffalo Bill's birthplace, of course, its Iowan origins forgotten now and its manner breezily indigenous. '*Cody Lives!*' cried a graffito I saw on a wall in town; and by golly, so he does.

Yet it came to me that the varnish was thin, and could be flaked away. There were often moments when the real and the spurious over-lapped, but they did not synthesize. I became aware that a gap separated the two, and that in Wyoming the communal self-delusion was at least incomplete. A distinction existed still, as it no longer did in New York, between the way people behaved privately, personally,

Wyoming

and the way they acted in their public personae. The transcendental-ism was in check. Self-awareness survived.

I sensed this first, unexpectedly, among townspeople, not in Cheyenne but in the smaller ranch and market towns which speckle the map of Wyoming. In area this is the ninth largest of the American States, but in population only Alaska is smaller. The 315,000 people of Wyoming are scattered among nearly 98,000 square miles of territory, so that miles of open country divide one little town from the next: aromatic, sage, snow and sunshine country, sprinkled at that time of the year with sweet small flowers, tracked by the hoofs of wandering cattle, bounded always by the distant line of Teton or Big Horn. Reaching a Wyoming town after a few hours' drive across the magnificent range is like reaching a particularly trim and comfortable oasis, for though it will naturally display most of the physical symp-toms of the American norm, still its isolation, and the beauty that surrounds it on every side, gives it a satisfying unity and compact-ness.

At one such place, Lander in Fremont County, I visited the Pioneer Museum, which is run by the county Pioneer Association. This body is presided over by dignitaries called the Esteemed Patri-arch and the Esteemed Matriarch, whose photographs hang honoured at the entrance, and the excellent small museum is attended by ladies scarcely less matriarchal or esteemable. During my visit a school-mistress was taking a group of children round the exhibits, and I heard her drawing their attention to a chair that stood in a corner of the gallery. It was made all of bleached white horn, legs, seat, back and all, and looked impressive but comfortless. 'That is an example', she was saying, 'of the craftsmanship of the very first pioneers to come to Fremont County. Isn't that beautiful, children?' Yes ma'am, most of them dutifully murmured, but after the main body had passed on to the Shoshone relics, a section of the museum I preferred to circumvent, I noticed a pair of laggard urchins trailing along behind. They had not heard their teacher's eulogy of the chair, but they too paused as they passed it, and inspected it with no less admiration. 'Jeez', one said to the other. 'Take a look at that Elk!'

I respected their expertise, and adopted their assessment as a synonym for the true in Wyoming. Elks abound in the State, and in all its homelier aspects I came to think of it as Elkin country. Elkin its splendour, elkin its charm, elkin I suspect its streak of country ruttishness, which tends to express itself in hawkish car stickers—

Wyoming

'*They'll take my gun away from me when my dead hands are too cold to hold it*', or '*I'm fighting poverty, I work.*' There is a kind of triumphal arch of elk antlers in the town square at Jackson, Wyoming, very apposite I thought, and it must have been elks they were referring to in a notice I saw upon a stockade near Pinedale: 'KEEP OUT, MEAN ANIMALS.'

The present Esteemed Patriarch of Lander, I was told, was by origin part English, part French, and part Sioux, and was the very first child ever to ride through town in a perambulator. These little Wyoming settlements are very new. The cliché that America itself is 'young' is, of course, preposterously out of date. It is one of the older nations now, and there are places in New England and the South that feel almost as ancient and stubborn as Little Ruttleborough on the Marsh. But this is one of the American hallucinations—the queer old-young flavour of it, the nation like so many of its matrons a weird cosmetic blend of decay, protean vigour, bluff and self-persuasion. Wyoming, though, needs no silitones. Wyoming really is young—a State since 1890—and Wyoming people talk about the original heroes of this frontier as we in Britain might recall well-remembered village characters of our childhood.

There was 'Old Lady' Boland, for instance, who ran a hotel in Lander for many years, who was well-known all over western Wyoming, and who crops up often in conversation still. What does Mrs. Ada Piper, 90, think of Old Lady Boland? 'Not much of a lady', says Mrs. Piper conclusively. Nobody is sacred in those parts, I was relieved to discover, and if I really tried I could even induce this citizenry to make disrespectful noises about Buffalo Bill. Butch Cassidy and the Wild Bunch, Cattle Kate, Flat Nose George the Train Robber—they remember them all without rancour or sentimentality, just ornery human critters like the rest of us, some good, some bad—'take Cattle Kate, now, they hanged her up there in Spring Creek Gulch, and some folks say she was real bad, but my Auntie Norah she knew her intimate, and she used to say there weren't nobody she'd sooner bake a pie with, not nobody. . . .'

I discovered in these little towns a kind of urbanity based not upon sophistication, but upon frankness. To the garage man, the laundry woman, the girl in the pharmacy, the motel reception clerk, there was an attitude of inquiry which much comforted me. Off the main road the Wyoming townsman still looks you straight and interested in the eye, as though not many strangers come his way. Make a remark and

Wyoming

he'll offer another. 'Look at your poor thumb', said I to a cobbler who was mending a strap for me, and whose thumb looked as though it had been, over several generations, repeatedly squashed in vices. 'You don't need to fret about it', he immediately replied, 'I give it a bang once in a while just to keep it awake.' In the post office at Medicine Bow, where Owen Wister set the immortal exchange of lines that culminated in 'When you call me that, *smile*'—in the false-fronted post office at Medicine Bow, almost next door to the Virginian Hotel and opposite the open range, the post-mistress gave me some handy advice about buying stamped envelopes. 'If you buy an envelope here I lick it for you, if you buy it some place else you do your own licking.' At Como Bluff, near a celebrated fossil field, there is a hut which claims itself to be the oldest building on earth, because it is made of fossilized dinosaur bones, and on this eccentric structure I saw a sign which trenchantly exemplified, I thought, the elkin directness of Wyoming: 'HONK HORN IF YOU WANT IN FOSSIL CABIN.'

The aristocrats of such a little town are the ranchers, in whose lives it plays the part that Andover, say, or Market Harborough play in the lives of country gentlemen in England. The cattle ranchers are the swells of Wyoming—they used often to be the villains, too, in the days when they ruthlessly harassed smallholders and sheepherders rash enough to settle in the territory. They live splendidly, many of them, in lovely country houses in the lee of the hills, with rose gardens and grand connections in the East—in England too, sometimes, for parts of Wyoming were settled by English milords.

I caught a pleasing glimpse of this society in the coffee-shop of a hotel at one mid-Wyoming town. The hotel lobby had not been encouraging. A fat, curled, eye-darkened, menacingly powdered moll eyed me unlovingly from the reception desk; chewing check-shirted figures leant against walls brooding; two or three reptilian elders with sticks and greasy Stetsons sat slumped in armchairs grunting; there was a clock on the wall with a face in the pattern of a Kennedy silver dollar, and a haze of cigar-smoke drifted among the apotheoses of Western life and re-enactments of Shoshone legend that hung upon the walls.

But I braved it all, and found a very different segment of society dominating the coffee-shop. The first thing that struck me about the group of ranchers lunching there was how fast they talked. That America contains more bores than all other countries put together is of course irrefutable: but it is not because Americans say boring things, only that they talk so slowly. This must reflect, I think, a fundamental defect of American educational method, for some of the slowest talkers and most excruciating bores of all, I have observed, have been Harvard men of exquisite instruction.

These Wyoming squires, though, talked fast, and with a nice mixture of cultivated and idiomatic English. They seemed altogether without self-consciousness: edgy, lean, rather brilliant people I thought. They struck me as *finished* men, who had never been reconstituted in the American melting-pot, but had always been themselves. Many of the Wyoming ranching families were certainly well-off from the start: early settlers around Sheridan, for instance, included English army officers who had first gone to the West buying horses for the British cavalry. The cattle barons of the 1880s and '90s were men of means and style—one of the first Powder River ranches was stocked at the beginning with 25,000 head of cattle—and when Theodore Roosevelt visited the State in 1910 he was given what was described as a characteristic Wyoming dinner: trout, pike, grouse, prairie chicken, roast elk with currant jelly, and champagne.

The ranchers still have a reputation for arrogance, but spared as they have been the miseries of the race struggle and the distortions of the social rat race, they seem to me more truly gentlemanly than most of the Virginia snobs or New England pedigree men who consider themselves the only American patricians. The men in the coffee-shop talked shop mostly, but it was marvellously racy or colourful shop: those darned heifers, getting the helicopter repaired, thirty miles of wire, Idaho mares, the Chinese grain market, 'if Ed says it's going to rain you can bet prime ribs it won't', and they parted, after coffee but no cigars, with courteous goodbyes to me and easy informalities to each other—'Thanks a lot', 'You bet, Sam', 'Be seein' ya', 'Love to Sue, now. . . .'

And so I came, circumspectly, to those theatrical archetypes of the American West, the cowboys. Much of the innocence had gone, I believed, with the decline of craftsmanship in the States, and with the consequent disappearance of a whole class of American working men —petty officer Americans, foremen Americans, the sort who never let you down, or forgot their tools. For a time the kind survived in the garage men of America, in the days when cars were still cherished as machinery, and American males appeared to have an instinctive

Wyoming

affinity with them. Some have been socially promoted, and are to be glimpsed grandly accoutred as the captains of American airliners. Some survive among my friends the New York harbour men. I have occasionally met one on a construction project far away, extending telecommunications in Persia or supervising the electrification of Siam. And a few thousand, I suppose, like Celts in Cornwall or pine martens in Wales, can be seen flourishing still in enclave, pure-bred and unmistakable, upon the ranges of Wyoming.

I approached them, as I say, with suspicion, for I feared the worst of them. Surely, after so many decades of the fancy, the rot had set in on the fact! But my very first encounter with Wyoming cowboys, on the road near Laramie, wonderfully reassured me. It seemed to me a genuinely romantic spectacle, in the grand manner. Their sheep and cattle were loitering in hundreds along the highway, straggling and nibbling up a hill, and the cowboys too seemed in no hurry at all. They did not nag. They were not fussed. They sat their horses with a divine assurance, all muscle, no bone, drooping rather, langorously chewing sometimes, with their Stetsons not too rakish, their gear moderately gaudy, and their posture one of lordly self-satisfaction. I loved them, and will not pretend to deny the frisson I derived from the elegant condescension of their greetings, as I nosed my car through the livestock and drove on aglow to Rock River.

The cowboys give to the Wyoming scene a style, at once sensual and aesthetic, to which most Americans are anxiously and I fear irrevocably alien. It was the cowboys, I realized now, not the redundant railwaymen or morose Arapahoes, who were the guardians of that lost identity: they, almost alone among their 180 million compatriots, still seemed at ease with their environment, their history, their jobs and themselves. Some of course are bad. They like guns and murder bald eagles. When they drive home from work in the evenings (for many now live in the towns), with their saddles in the backs of their cars, their mode does slightly shift away from High Chapparal towards Easy Rider. They often wear dark glasses, too, which gives them a slightly sinister air. But in casual encounter and conversation there can be no gentler or more polished working men. They are the nearest thing to a white American peasantry, I suppose, and they possess a timeless rural grace.

Often these magnificent people befriended me. Once they invited me to come on down and watch the branding: and I left the car, and scrambled down the bank to the fence below, and there I found an

Wyoming

Indianified cowboy very slowly walking his horse around an enclosure lassoing bullocks by their hind legs—a performance of some
grandeur, almost stately, with a measured tread of the horse and a
theatrical swank to the tilt of the horseman's head. One by one he
picked his steers and dragged them, helplessly kicking, over to the
branding pit, where heat sizzled from oxygen cylinders, the air smelt
of scorched flesh, and a couple of elderly ranch-hands nonchalantly
branded them. They greeted me rather as stall-holders welcome passing visitors to village fêtes—graciously, that is, almost protectively,
and informatively. Stall-holders are inclined to tell you about dry-rot
in the church tower, or trace the ancestry of Sir Charles at the Manor.
Cowboys put you in the picture about cattle. 'Take the Lazy Y Brand,
that means a letter Y lying on its side, see, kinda layabout. U Lazy A,
that means a letter U and a sideways A. The Hildebrand outfit, they
brand Upside Y Lazy 3—that's a letter Y upside down and a number
3 backside up. We have all sorts—E Slash 4, Lazy Diamond R—you
get the hang of it in time, same as you get the hang of most anything. . . .'

   Or sometimes they merely walked their horses up to me, as I
picnicked in the sage, or sat sketching in my car, or took my morning
walk through the scented countryside, picking flowers for my notebook or trying to analyse the dappled colour-patterns on the hills:
and then, after we had exchanged pleasantries, and told each other
where we came from, and explained what we were doing, sometimes
they would slide lithe from their saddles and join me for a few minutes,
looking over my shoulder at a sketch, accepting a slice of cheese, or
simply sharing the pleasure of the place and the moment—not a
talkative presence usually, but one so natural, kind and unembarras-
sed that a silence was never awkward, and the parting came organically, like the end of a good meal, just before satisfaction moved
towards surfeit.

This reminded me very much of Spain: and just as in Spain, in the
bitterest expanses of the high *meseta*, the Spaniard commands the
scene with his dignity, so it seemed to me that the cowboys in Wyoming, with their Castilian tact and splendour, needed no pretence.
They were themselves, uncompromised. I thought it a happy irony,
in the end, that I seemed to have found the last American reality in
the very ark of the American myth.